A
SYSTEMS APPROACH
TO
COMMUNITY COLLEGE
EDUCATION

A
SYSTEMS APPROACH
TO
COMMUNITY COLLEGE
EDUCATION

DAVID E. BARBEE

EDUCATION AND TRAINING CONSULTANT

AUERBACH®
publishers

princeton
philadelphia
new york
london

Library of Congress Catalog Card Number: 73-189534
International Standard Book Number: 0-87769-124-X

First Printing

Printed in the United States of America

Contents

Preface

My purposes in writing this book are to bring to persons interested in education, and particularly in community college education, alternatives to the present nonresponsive organization of the institution as manifested at all levels of education, from the kindergarten through the graduate school. The alternative developed and presented is based on a philosophy of education and theories of instruction and curriculum that are syntheses of the findings, ideas, and developments of many individuals.

I have included a set of guidelines (Chapter 7) developed for a community college administrator, but equally applicable to any educator or layman interested in improving education. These guidelines describe how a person interested in improving education may employ the process of technology—the systems approach—in solving educational problems.

If you have questions or ideas you would like to explore further after reading this book, please address them to me at P.O. Box 788, Aspen, Colorado 81611.

Acknowledgments

The ideas expressed in this book represent the thinking of many persons far too numerous to mention individually. However, several persons stand out as major contributors and influences. Dr. Thomas Gilbert and Dr. B. F. Skinner, Dr. Lloyd Homme and Dr. David Premack, the late Dr. Norbert Wiener, Dr. Karl U. Smith and Dr. Margaret Foltz Smith, the late Dr. John Dewey, Dr. Jerome Bruner and Dr. John Goodlad, the late Drs. John Franklin Bobbitt, Boyd Bode, and W. W. Charters, Dr. Hilda Taba, Dr. Gabriel D. Ofiesh, and Dr. Francis Mechner, Dr. Leonard Silvern, Dr. Sam Postlethwait and Dr. John Tirrell. Many of the ideas expressed here may be attributed to Dr. Aubrey J. Bouck, without whose assistance and support this book would not have been possible.

To Dr. John Tirrell, Ted Pohrte, Art Schmidt, Dr. Oliver Lane, Dr. Elbie Gann, and the many others at Colorado Mountain College and other institutions whose inputs were of great value, goes my appreciation.

My very special thanks to Mary my wife and my children, Mark, Michael, and Mary Elizabeth, for their patience, understanding, and help.

1

Introduction

Dr. Edmund J. Gleazer, Jr., executive secretary of the American Association of Junior Colleges, has said of the comprehensive community college:

> This institution is an American Social Invention. It is an instrument of tremendous potential. It can motivate youth who have had little hope for learning beyond high school. It can lift the sights and strengthen the efforts of the generation wanting to go beyond their fathers' achievements. It can stimulate the creativity and slumbering interests of adults. It can provide the means for training that lead to a higher level of employment. It can train for the new skills demanded by a changing technology. It can serve as a focal point for community identification. Oriented to the community, controlled by the community, it can be the catalyst for the processes by which the values of a free world's culture can be refined and advanced.[1]

To meet the challenge posed by the creation of this two-year open-door institution, bold new approaches are required. Community colleges are charged with the responsibility for meeting not only the educational needs of youth but also the intellectual, vocational, and continuing needs of all members of the community. To service these varied needs represents a substantial challenge for this new, uniquely American, institution. After you carefully analyze the needs, it should become apparent that the instructional program of the college must be individualized, that is, it must meet the needs of each individual and thus the collective needs of the community.

To further complicate the problem, the needs of the community are constantly changing in our dynamic society; new knowledge that is useful

1

in designing more efficient and effective learning experiences is being acquired on a continuing basis. With this state of flux and taxpayers demanding more efficient use of resources, a way of approaching these challenges must be found that will help this fledgling institution realize its full potential.

There are also some real educational needs:

11,000,000 Americans of age eighteen and older cannot read or write. The United States Office of Education estimates that of the 30,000,000 boys and girls who will be seeking jobs in this decade, 2,000,000 will not have seen the inside of a high school, and 7,000,000—nearly one-fourth—will not finish high school.[2]

This is not to say that those who have attended high school have no educational needs.

It is becoming increasingly clear that the junior college will be called upon to assume sharply increasing responsibility as enrollments in higher education skyrocket during the years immediately ahead. Junior college enrollments now approach one and a quarter million and are expected to double, or even treble within the next decade. This expansion will inevitably be accompanied by a demand for greater efficiency in all aspects of operations—an efficiency that will make it possible for junior colleges to offer high quality instruction to unprecedented numbers of students at a cost commensurate with that which society is able and willing to pay. Taxpayers and private donors to higher education can be expected to insist upon getting the highest possible value for every dollar spent on colleges and universities.[3]

What is the community or junior college to do to meet this challenge? Obviously it must create more of itself and grow in numbers of students educated, *but it must do more*. What is going on now?

The community college must employ a more systematic approach to meeting the challenges of increased efficiency and effectiveness in establishing and meeting institutional goals.

More than 1000 community or junior colleges exist and at least one new community or junior college is being established in the United States each week. While most are instructional carbon copies of other junior colleges, a few in recent years have broken with this tradition and have sought new models. Some have attempted to employ more systematic approaches to the development of their student-centered instructional program.[4]

One of these institutions is Oakland Community College. In September 1965 it opened the doors of its two campuses to 3,800 full-time students in Oakland County, Michigan. Oakland's president, Dr. John Tirrell, contrasted his approach to the more conventional approaches to instruction:

> . . . Oakland Community College has attempted to develop an instructional approach which is primarily learner-centered. This Learner-Centered Instructional Program is an outgrowth of the systems approach to education and training in general. The overall concern with human learning, training and educational research fostered after World War II by such organizations as are now represented by the United States Army Human Resources Research Office (HumRRO), United States Air Force Behavioral Sciences Laboratory, American Institute for Research, and others, has promoted the advancement of the State-of-the-Art for educational and training technology. Oakland Community College has recognized these advancements and availed itself of this technology. Developments in programmed learning itself have, of course, influenced the Oakland Community College concept profoundly. Most recently, the work of Dr. S. N. Postlethwait of the Botany Department at Purdue University has provided a working model (The Audio-Tutorial Method) from which the instructional Systems Approach at Oakland Community College was initially derived. The Oakland Community College approach has now been modified to the point that the term "Audio-Tutorial" is no longer used.[5]

Tirrell summarizes by saying ". . . The purpose of the approach at Oakland was to reach more students with less instructional personnel, promote the learning of more information with greater comprehension and in less time."[6]

B. Lamar Johnson found other community colleges using the audio-tutorial approach developed by Dr. Sam Postlethwait of Purdue University. Some of these predate Oakland, such as the Junior College District of St. Louis, Meramec Community College, Florissant Valley Community College, and Forest Park Community College. Others, including 13 colleges in California and at least 20 more institutions around the country, are using this approach in one or more courses.[7]

Although Dr. Johnson equates audio-tutorial methodology with a systems approach to instruction, it was implemented principally as a teaching methodology.

In order to develop more efficient and effective systems for meeting educational needs, more than a new teaching methodology is required. The implementation of a completely new process is required, which is called a "systems approach."

In this book I have attempted to show how this process may be employed at all levels in the community college to meet the challenge stated at the beginning of this chapter.

Just what is the "systems approach"? It is the application of a rigorous, iterative process that must include the following:

1. A clear description of goals and objectives is necessary as they provide the basis for
   a. the initial specification of *required resources*
   b. the *trade-off* analysis of potential solutions
   c. the *evaluation* of performance
2. A clear definition of constraints is necessary because it establishes the conditions within which the system must function.
3. The establishment of measures of effectiveness, which simply means what will be accepted as a measure of having achieved the objectives or as a measure of the degree to which the objectives have been achieved.
4. The synthesis of alternate solutions consists of hypothesizing different ways of achieving the objectives within the specified constraints, considering all significant aspects of the problem, i.e., consideration of the problems of designing, fabricating, implementing, testing, evaluating, revising, and operating the system.
5. In the establishment of cost elements, *all* costs and their amortization over the period of anticipated utilization are considered in order to provide a basis for comparisons between the proposed alternate approaches to achieving the objectives.
6. A cost versus effectiveness type of analysis is initiated in order to make trade-off decisions between alternative solutions. The solution that creates the best possible education for the least cost is sought. Since a limited budget is a reality true of all community college education, it is important to get the most student learning for the dollars invested.
7. The continuing process of evaluation after the system has been implemented involves utilization of feedback (empirical evidence) as a basis for modification of the system.

The systems approach is not a sequential series of steps; it is a dynamic, iterative process. Initial objectives are modified as a result of later analysis; constraints may be modified as a result of seeing their impact on the cost of the system; the proposed solutions will be modified as a result of trade-off studies; the entire system may be redesigned as a result of the operational evaluation. Hence, at every step of the way, the results are analyzed to verify or modify earlier decisions.[8]

This is the process that must be applied to education to enable us to meet educational needs.

In order to fully understand how a systems approach can be applied, one must explore the emerging theories of instruction and curriculum and trace the history of the application of a systems approach to instruction.

Specifically, in Chapter 2, I have drawn together the thoughts of a number of persons to put together the beginnings of a theory of instruction. This theory is drawn from the behavioral sciences and their applications and from the field of cybernetics.

In Chapter 3 I make a similar attempt to identify an emerging theory of curriculum. First, I survey the state-of-the-art in curriculum, then make an historical analysis of scientific approaches to curriculum development, and finally explore the state of development of a theory of curriculum.

Chapter 4 describes the emergence of a philosophy of education including instruction and curriculum; conclusions are drawn based on Chapters 2, 3, and 4. I must admit that in these first four chapters I feel a bit like the former in: "fools rush in where angels fear to tread."

In Chapter 5 I trace historically the application of the systems approach to instruction, describe programs presently employing elements of the approach, and finally propose an instructional systems model that has been synthesized from existing models.

Chapter 6 outlines some of the pitfalls that may be encountered in employing a systems approach to instruction and overall institutional development by describing what happened in one institution. In this chapter I have attempted to describe the situation as I feel it is, because too often, reports of projects do not tell the whole story, they do not make explicit the problems encountered so that others may profit from their experience. If any institution is to remain vital and healthy, it must learn from its mistakes and the mistakes of others.

In Chapter 7 I develop specific guidelines for the community college educator wishing to adopt a systems approach to the solution of his problems.

A glossary and an extensive bibliography follow Chapter 7.

2

An Emerging Theory
of Instruction

In an article written in 1967, Myron Lieberman points out an interesting paradox:

> Just why we accept the need for a systems approach to putting a man on the moon but not for educating millions of persons annually is an interesting paradox. The mythology that sustains this paradox includes the notions that technology will dehumanize education, that it will transform teachers from professionals into mere technicians, and that it has no use or relevance for the value-oriented aspects of education.[1]

Perhaps Hilda Taba has put her finger on the problem:

> We call those who make technical changes inventors, but those who make changes in nonmaterial culture are likely to be called rebels, revolutionaries, and reformers, words which do not carry a positive flavor in the American mind. Neither is our culture predisposed toward planning social change, whereas planned technological change is commonplace.[2]

Jerome Bruner has said that man is dependent upon technology for his very humanity:

> Man's use of mind is dependent upon his ability to develop and use "tools" or "instruments" or "technologies" that make it possible for him to express and amplify his powers. . . . It was not a large-brained hominid that developed the technical-social life of the human; rather it was the tool-using, cooperative pattern that gradually changed man's mor-

7

phology by favoring the survival of those who could link themselves with tool systems and disfavoring those who tried to go it on big jaws, heavy dentition, or superior weight. What evolved as a human nervous system was something, then, that required outside devices for expressing its potential. . . . *Man is then dependent upon tools and technology for his very humanity.*[3] (Emphasis mine.)

In order to develop a model for an instructional program that takes full advantage of the findings made during this century in the basic areas of psychology, sociology, anthropology, physics, biochemistry and myriad other sciences, it is necessary to study their applications to practical problems. The application of this information to the practical problems facing education is termed *educational technology*. As the well-known economist, John Kenneth Galbraith, has said: "Technology means the systematic application of scientific or other organized knowledge to practical tasks."[4]

As an example, when reinforcement or any other theory of behavior is applied to education, the medium is behavioral *technology*, or when information theory is applied to education, the medium is information *technology*.

The basic *process* of all technologies is the same—it is the *systems approach*. Technology, whether applied to education or to sending men to Mars, is a *process*. It has no content; it is not a discipline and it is not the product that is derived by the process.

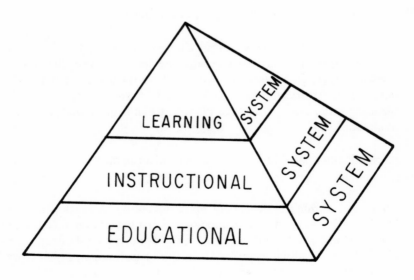

To increase the probability of success in designing an instructional program or any other program, it is necessary to apply existing knowledges through the medium of technology, using the systems approach.

A RATIONALE

The central focus of all educational endeavor must be on the learner. The teacher in the classroom, the book on the shelf, the 16mm projector in the closet, the dean in the office, the Commissioner of Education in Washington, and even the professors of education, wherever they are, all exist for one reason and that is to effect student learning in a predetermined manner. This notion may be visualized by thinking of a pyramid, the apex of which is the student interacting with his environment so that he learns what it has been determined should be learned. This is the *learning system*—the individual student interacting with a prestructured responsive environment.

Below the apex, representing a band through the middle of the pyramid, is the *instructional system*, consisting of other resources (teachers, deans, media specialists, counselors, and clerks) who make up the learning environments, along with the management and logistic support of such environments. Each component of this instructional system exists solely to facilitate the learning system and as a consequence supports it in the same way that the middle section of any pyramid supports its apex.

At the bottom of the pyramid is the *educational system*, which comprises the support for clusters of instructional systems (transportation, central business and administrative functions, capital construction, etc.) and facilitates the operation of the *instructional system*, which in turn serves the *learning system*, which exists only to optimize student learning.

However, on closer inspection we find, unfortunately, that the educational pyramid has been constructed upside down, apparently for the following reasons:

1. A comprehensive theory of instruction is lacking in educational planning. This is true even though the ingredients of such a theory exist, based upon two fundamental principles of behavior: (a) *the human being continually modifies his behavior,* therefore the natural state of man, by definition, is learning (modification of behavior); and (b) *the human being's behavior is determined by his perception of the consequences of that behavior.*

2. The current answers to the following two questions are mortally deficient: What is the real value placed on learning by the society? Does the society have confidence in the educational system, as it exists, to produce learning? The answers to these questions, respectively, would have to be a speculative "little" and a definite "no."

A THEORY OF INSTRUCTION EMERGES

I have used the word "theory" to refer to "the coherent set of hypothetical, conceptual, and pragmatic principles forming the general frame of reference for a field of inquiry. . . ."[5] A theory of instruction should include both a theory of learning and a theory of teaching. Until recent years, however, the bulk of pedagogical effort has centered on the teacher and the methodology. Bruner has said: "Instruction is . . . an effort to assist or to shape growth. And a theory of instruction . . . is . . . a theory of how growth and development are assisted by diverse means."[6] Bruner and many others have said that the single most characteristic thing about people is that they *learn*, or as William James put it decades ago, "Even our instinctive behavior occurs only once, thereafter being modified by experience."[7]

Now let's see how this single principle can form the basis not only of a theory of learning but of a fairly comprehensive theory of instruction, while at the same time remembering Bruner's caution: "I can only hope that in pursuing a theory of instruction we shall have the courage to recognize what we do not understand and to permit ourselves a new and innocent look."[8]

There have been some attempts in learning and instructional-system design to develop a technology of instruction based on as complete a theory of instruction as exists, one that is capable of answering; What ought to be taught? How? To whom? When?[9] Although the various theories of learning have little in common beyond the fact that a person does learn, a theory of teaching has emerged that is based on principles developed through research. Davies put it this way:

. . . We are at last in sight of a theory of teaching, a guide to pedagogy, rather than being overly dependent on a theory of learning. . . . The kind of theory that is being envisaged here is one that looks upon teaching as the "independent variable." Such an approach makes it possible to deal with a whole class of phenomena hitherto neglected by learning theorists, and makes possible a science of teaching with a technology of its very own.[10]

This theory of teaching is known as praxeonomy and was based on the earlier development of mathetics. The developer of both was Dr. Thomas F. Gilbert. Before discussing this specific technology let's review the development of behavioral science on which it is based.

Behavioral Science

It was B. F. Skinner who made the study of behavior objective; he created the science of behavior, the foundations of which were laid by Watson, Pavlov, and Thorndike in the early 1900s. Watson may be said to have changed psychology from the study of the mind to the study of behavior. Pavlov's significant contribution was in the realm of classical conditioning.[11]

Thorndike, in studying the interaction of the organism with its environment under rigorously controlled conditions and using objective measures of behavior, developed these principles:

1. behavior that is reinforced tends to occur again;
2. behavior that is not reinforced tends to disappear;
3. mere repetition of behavior does not necessarily strengthen it.

Perhaps Thorndike's greatest contribution, however, was in developing a methodology—the beginnings of a technology of behavior.[12]

I believe it was Skinner's contributions, beginning in the 1930s and continuing today in his work at Harvard, that catalyzed the development of a science of behavior. He made the study of behavior truly objective. His work, *The Behavior of Organisms*,[13] was the turning point in the study of behavior; it detailed a new methodology for its experimental analysis.

Many volumes could be devoted to Skinner's many and varied contributions to the field, both in the development of the science at the basic (theoretical) level and in the applications of the basic science at the technological or engineering level.

Professor Herrustein, a former student of Skinner's and now chairman of Harvard's psychology department, said in an interview with the *New*

York Times in 1968: "The trouble with Fred . . . is he keeps skipping over from basic science into technological applications of his theories, like teaching machines."[14] In addition to his teaching machines, Skinner also developed applications such as an "air crib," a controlled but responsive environment in which a baby may play without the restriction of clothing or blankets. Even his *Walden Two* transcends basic science; it could certainly be classed as an attempt at the engineering of human behavior.[15]

Others, for example Keller, applied behavior principles to teaching, and developed programs that were more efficient than previous instruction.[16] Again in the early 1950s, Skinner showed how his principles could be applied by developing programmed instructional sequences and teaching machine technology. Perhaps this is the very reason Skinner has been such an influence and why he may stand as one of the scientific giants of this century.

During the 1950s a behavioral technology gradually began to be applied, principally to training systems, in industry and government. This technology of behavior asserts that since it is not possible within the present state of the art to observe directly whether a person possesses certain knowledges or understandings, what he does (behavior) must be accepted as evidence that learning has taken place. Therefore it is necessary to establish beforehand quite specifically what behavior (performance) will be accepted as evidence that the student has learned what he was supposed to have learned. The stimulus conditions under which the performance is to take place, as well as the accuracy or level of performance, are also specified.

In 1964 Mechner and Cook summarized the approach a behavioral technologist takes to a problem in these steps:

1. He specifies the behavior the student is to acquire (where behavior may be evidence of knowledge).
2. He specifies the relevant characteristics of the student, including the student's present level of knowledge.
3. He performs a behavioral analysis on the material to be taught. This involves "atomizing" the knowledge to be imparted according to learning theory principles. The knowledge is broken down into concepts, discriminations, generalizations, and chains.
4. He constructs a teaching system or program by which the behavior may be built into the student's repertoire. In constructing this system

or program, he decides on the techniques most suitable for the problem at hand.

5. He tests the teaching system on sample students and revises it according to the results, until the desired result is reliably achieved in student after student.[17]

The behavioral technologist must be concerned with more. Also in 1964, Homme needled training personnel about ignoring the known principles in dealing with human behavior. He offered as an explanation the fact that conventional reinforcers are weak compared with the common animal reinforcer—food to a hungry animal. He offers the *Premack Principle*, "Any behavior can be reinforced by following it with a behavior of higher probability," as the principle to apply to the solution of this problem. Discovered by David Premack at the University of Missouri in 1959, this principle was equated in importance by Homme with the discovery of gravity.[18] Homme as variously described the concept as "Grandma's Law"; "Eat your ham and beans" (lower probability behavior), "then you may have dessert" (higher probability behavior); or the "First work, then play" rule. He even points out nature's uses of the principle: ". . . The carnivorous wild animal *must* hunt (lower probability behavior) before he gets to eat (higher probability behavior)."[19] In spite of this relatively simple concept, Homme cites perhaps more frequent examples of reversal of contingencies: "One more game of cards (or something else that was fun), then you've *got* to do your homework." In other words, stop that high probability behavior and then you may come and do this low probability behavior.[20]

The essential difference between the postulates of Skinner and those of Premack lies in the size and nature of the reinforcer. Premack identified larger reinforcers through the identification of high probability behavior. But neither man has taken the next step consistent with pragmatic instructional requirements, and said: "I don't want to use just observed high probability behaviors as reinforcers; I want to create others that are more readily under my control, require less resources, or are operable within my constraints." Since reinforcers are stimuli that elicit predictable responses that are satisfying (high probability of occurrence) to the learner, the problem becomes one of shaping the behavior of the learner in such a way that less satisfying responses become more satisfying. To accomplish this, the same techniques are employed as in other behavior modification.

There were a few highly successful examples of behavioral technology applied to human behavior during the 1960s. For a demonstration of a successful trial, see Cohen's Cases I and II.[21] Most trials were successful, but they were few compared with the enormity of the training and educational problem.

To restate the behavioral principles applicable to management that were available or developed in the 1960s:

1. Positive consequences are more valuable in maintaining a specific behavior than negative consequences are in extinguishing a behavior.
2. A lower probability behavior may be reinforced by one of higher probability.
3. The value of a reinforcer varies from one individual to another and from one time to another.[22]
4. Success is not always reinforcing; in fact, students who have a high achievement motivation relax after a success and show heightened motivation after a failure experience.[23]
5. Knowledge of results is most effective when goals are specifically defined for a student and are related to his need for achievement.[24]

With this background in behavioral science, now return with me to praxeonomy and Dr. Gilbert.

PRAXEONOMY

When persons are not performing as anticipated, it is usually attributed to lack of training. In reality, nothing could be further from the truth. There is more than one way of overcoming human deficiencies, and training is seldom the best. This concept forms the basis for "praxeonomy," which is a philosophy and a systematic way of identifying real training needs.[25]

In order to better understand this notion, let's examine Gilbert's concept of "performance deficiency." In this concept a basic discrimination between the two aspects of achievement, *accomplishment* and *acquirement*, is required. "Acquirement refers to what a person has learned; whereas, accomplishment refers to the outcome, or the effect, of what a person has learned on his performance."[26]

To illustrate this concept, I have drawn an example from *A Guide to Analyzing Instructional Needs*, a manual recently published by the U.S. Forest Service.

SITUATION: Tom, Dick, and Harry are students in the fifth grade. They are given a test in long division, a subject in which they have all received instruction.

The test has very high reliability and validity, and the stamp of approval of 50 licensed psychologists. It is administered under the most carefully controlled conditions, and all three boys are at the peak of their attention.

SAMPLE
PROBLEM: Here is a typical problem in the test in long division:

$$26 \div 12$$

(Carry the answer to 2 decimal places.)

CORRECT
ANSWER: Obviously, the correct answer to this problem is:

$$
\begin{array}{r}
2.16 \\
12\overline{\smash{\big)}26.00} \\
24 \\
\overline{2\,0} \\
1\,2 \\
\overline{80} \\
72 \\
\overline{8} = \text{remainder}
\end{array}
$$

Now turn to the following page, and see how Tom, Dick, and Harry each answered this problem.

R E A C T I O N S

TOM	DICK	HARRY

```
        2.18                        2                      .46
   12 | 26.00               12 |   26              26 | 12.00
        24                         24                    10 4
        ──                         ──                    ────
        2 0                         2 = remainder        1 60
        1 2                                              1 56
        ───                                              ────
        1 00                                                4 = remainder
          96
        ────
        1 00 = remainder
```

CHECK what each boy knows about long division. (If the problem does not illustrate whether the boy has learned an item listed on the right, place a check mark in the box below his name.)

Tom   Dick   Harry

□   □   □   1. Difference between dividend and divisor.
□   □   □   2. How to set up the problem.
□   □   □   3. How to point off decimal places.
□   □   □   4. How to subtract whole numbers.
□   □   □   5. How to subtract whole numbers from zeros.
□   □   □   6. How to multiply.
□   □   □   7. How to carry in subtraction and multiplication.
□   □   □   8. What to do if the subtraction results in a remainder which the divisor goes into less than one whole time.
□   □   □   9. Where to place the products and remainders.
□   □   □   10. Where to write the answer.

PLACE a check mark by each statement below that is a sensible conclusion from the descriptions above.

□   Tom, Dick, and Harry each know about equally as much long division.

□   A small difference in knowledge can make a big difference in effect.

OVERALL RESULTS

Tom and Dick each scored 50% on the test, and Harry made a zero. Not very praiseworthy accomplishments!

The obvious interpretation is that Tom and Dick are individuals who do not differ, and each knows half of what he needs to know in order to perform problems in long division correctly. Harry, on the other hand, clearly doesn't know a thing about long division.

Yet the illustration of how each boy answered the sample problem shown on the previous page indicates that all three can perform approximately 99% of the operations of long division accurately. Both Tom and Dick came close to getting the correct answer, but neither one was able to complete the problem satisfactorily. And each boy was unable to do so for entirely different reasons.

Tom does not know how to subtract a whole number from a zero, whereas Dick does not know what to do if the subtraction results in a remainder which the divisor goes into less than one whole time. For this reason, we don't know whether or not he knows how to point off decimal places.

Harry's answer was far from correct. Yet he knows how to perform every operation perfectly except one. He makes the error of putting the dividend outside the long division bracket and the divisor inside. And this one incorrect operation leads to a much bigger difference in outcome than the results of the errors which the other two boys make.

Tom hasn't learned all the prerequisites for learning long division, whereas Dick hasn't learned all the operations of long division. Harry, on the other hand, has learned all the prerequisites, and he has also learned all the operations—except one.

Harry's deficiency would be the simplest to correct, but since it applies to every problem, it appears to be the most enormous. Tom's and Dick's deficiencies are much more serious. However, they appear much less so because they don't matter in every problem—only half of them. They also appear to be identical because each boy scored 50%. Yet Tom missed some problems which Dick answered correctly. They each missed the same problems only when those same problems required the particular operations that each individual boy couldn't perform.

FURTHER OBSERVATIONS

To complete the demonstration, let's suppose that the test is given to Harry's twin brother. Like Harry, Harry's twin knows all the prerequisites. However, unlike Harry, he also knows all the operations, including where to place the dividend and divisor before dividing. Therefore, his score on the achievement test is 100%.

The test has made the great difference between what Tom and Dick have each acquired, or learned, look small. At the same time, it has also made the small difference between what Harry and his twin brother have each learned, or acquired, seem like a great difference.

THE PARADOX

Tests of achievement present a paradox. On the one hand, they obscure individual differences; and on the other, they seem to magnify and exaggerate individual differences.

However, a paradox exists only when we are talking about two different things as if they were one and the same. This is precisely the cause of the problem in this instance. However, there is a solution to the paradox.

SOLUTION

We need to understand that there are two ways in which repertoires of human knowledge can differ:

    a. in what is acquired;

    b. in what is accomplished.

Tests can be sensitive to one, but not to the other, for they can do one of two things:

    a. measure the number of operations missing from, or existing in, a behavior repertory;

    b. measure the effects a behavior repertory has on the environment.

For the latter purpose, the long division test is nearly perfect and of great potential use. But, for the former purpose, it is useless and indeed, damaging and downright subversive to the ends of instruction.

Harry scored zero on the test. Yet he knew 99% of the operations of long division. If the test was measuring what he knew about long division, or the number of operations in his repertory, he would have scored 99. Clearly, the test was not measuring the operations of mastery which Harry had acquired.

It was, however, measuring the effect, or the outcome, of Harry's behavior repertory. Recall that the test score reflected a count of the number of correctly completed problems.

For all of Harry's skill in long division, he was unable to produce the final product required of mastery. His achievement was as useless as that of one who had achieved nothing at all. He had acquired much, but accomplished nothing.

Although the long division test is called an achievement test, it is clearly one of accomplishment. Like most so-called achievement tests it confounds the two aspects of individual differences.

CONCLUSIONS

This discussion of the confusion about what is meant by achievement leads to the following conclusions:

1. Individual differences in acquirement are much smaller than we are used to assuming they are.
2. Therefore, it follows that student deficiencies in acquirement are much smaller than we usually assume.
3. The greatest individual differences are in accomplishment.

The importance of these concepts, acquirement and accomplishment, is that they underly the four rules used in limiting the objectives that are the basis for instruction:

1. Remove from a list of potential objectives any skills in which the employee is *not* deficient; in other words, make a determination of what *needs* to be taught, not what might or could be taught.
2. In order to do this, the student's performance before instruction is measured in terms of acquirement, not accomplishment. (Remember, *acquirement* refers to what the student has learned and *accomplishment* refers to the outcome.)
3. Once this has been established for each student, then each behavior must be studied to distinguish between those that represent deficiencies of *knowledge* (he doesn't know how to do it) and those representing deficiencies of *execution* (he knows how, but just doesn't do it for one reason or another).
4. Establish the instructional priorities by determining whether or not the value of overcoming the deficiency is greater than the cost incurred.[27]

If in the final analysis, it is determined that training is necessary, i.e., there is a deficiency in acquirement between the student's and the master's performance and the deficiency is one of knowledge, then we may turn to the most comprehensive technology of education yet developed—mathetics.

Mathetics

Davies has said that mathetics, when combined with the Premack principle,[28] offers, "a complete theory of teaching (instruction)." Mathetics doesn't represent just another point of view, instructional method, or programming technique; rather, "it is an authoritative scientific technology. Indeed, mathetics has been described as the technology of education, since it is a systematic way of planning the course of human learning."[29]

A matheticist categorizes behavior as chains, multiples, discriminations, or generalizations. Each receives a different prescriptive treatment based only on the category, not the content.

Dr. Gilbert, the developer of this technology (praxeonomy-mathetics), earned his Ph.D. at Harvard University under Professor B. F. Skinner. Writing in the *Journal of Mathetics* in 1962, Gilbert said: "Mathetics may be defined as the systematic application of reinforcement theory to the analysis and reconstruction of those complex behavior repertoires usually known as 'subject-matter mastery,' 'knowledge,' and 'skill.' "[30]

As with all technologies, a rigorous process is employed. There are three tasks necessary in designing an effective learning environment based on mathetics:

1. An analysis of the required behaviors.
2. An exercise that translates the analysis into materials appropriate to the learner and the task.
3. A description of the learning problems these behaviors are likely to present.

The matheticist views the instructional problem as a "teaching problem," which he solves by determining what steps a student must take in order to achieve mastery of a subject or skill and arrange the stimulus conditions so as to insure that the student will take these steps. He does this by selectively reinforcing appropriate learner behavior. Since most, if not all, behaviors already exist in the repertoire of the learner, it is the task of the matheticist to rearrange the learner's repertoire. This is done by coupling new stimuli with existing responses, or vice versa, and by resequencing chains.

The matheticist produces a lesson plan (not to be confused with the typical lesson plan) which forms the basis for the design of the learning environment (configuration of the materials). There are four stages in developing this plan: (1) task analysis, (2) prescription, (3) domain theory, (4) characterization.[31] These stages, once completed, form the basis for the design of the exercises for tryout and editing. So precise and replicable is the analysis and writing that "two matheticists working independently on the same subject matter will produce lessons that are virtually identical in all essential respects."[32] (If the reader is interested in pursuing this topic further, I would suggest that he write directly to Dr. Thomas Gilbert, President, Praxis, 47 W. 13th St., New York, N.Y. 10011.)

Gilbert's work has largely been overlooked by educators; even many psychologists have rejected it, perhaps because of its direct lineage to studies of animal behavior. Dr. James L. Evans has listed several reasons for the lack of acceptance, other than the fact that the studies have never been widely disseminated or publicized, in sum: the claims made for mathetics strike some as presumptuous; the system is rigidly behavioristic; Gilbert has a penchant for giving new names to old ideas and old names to new ideas; and finally, he often fails to exemplify many of his key concepts.[33] Gilbert himself may have shed some additional light on the problem when he said:

In education, individual differences among behavior repertories are usually difficult to discuss with detachment, simply because they are confused with the value we place upon human individuality. The issue is much simpler if we agree that an educational technology is applicable only to animal behavior, that man is at least an animal, and that differences among men's animal skills could be totally obliterated without affecting the differences in the way they choose to use them.

It seems to me that much of the fear that individuality will be destroyed if we teach all men the same skills arises from an uncritical equation of the ability to perform and the decision to perform. Art schools have more and more avoided teaching traditional skills presumably to protect the student's creativity, which I take to mean his decision to use his skills in unusual combinations.[34]

We seem to be so afraid of losing our supposed freedom. I think Dr. Evans, commenting in "The Technology of Doing Your Own Thing," has shown why the use of technology will help us to *secure* our freedom.

Freedom in Summerhill is not true freedom, because it lacks instructional technology. In Summerhill there is no library of behaviorally designed self-instructional material, no computer-assisted instruction, no immediate data retrieval, no access to the multitudes of existing audio-visual material; there is no system of self-management that will ensure a steady, if not necessarily an orderly, progression toward ultimate freedom—not the false freedom of doing your own thing. We are able to do anything we want to do only when we have paid for this freedom by doing our (nonmutually-exclusive) scientific and humanistic homework.

Responding only to the most immediate stimuli does not necessarily constitute doing one's own thing; it is evident from the unhappy record book on those who have chosen to flee from society as it is normally constituted and do their own things in places such as Haight-Ashbury that it is not quite that simple. It is a difficult thing to measure, but is likely that the percentage of those who have really "found their own thing and done it," whatever that means, is low.

But we no longer need, in this electric age, to be so handicapped in allowing random and potentially invidious variables to determine how we choose our own thing. Now that we have a technology of data collection, reduction, and retrieval, we can provide anyone who really wants to do his own thing with almost unlimited information about arts, sciences, humanities, and crafts in living color and stereophonic sound. The person who knows no thing (nothing) has no choice; the person who knows one thing has two choices, whether to do it or not; the person who knows two things has four choices, whether to do the first choice, the second choice, both choices, or neither choices. And so on in binary fashion. From this analysis it is easy to see that we have a geometric approach to freedom (being able to do your thing) that is based on knowing things, and not knowing nothing. If one's thing is geometry, one may only be able to name the five Platonic Solids. If one's thing is brazing pieces of coat hangers into art objects, then one can pursue that activity. But if one knows about the five Platonic Solids *and* brazing coat hangers, he can construct, if he wants to, the five solid geometric figures out of brazed coat hanger bits. If, further, he knows the laws of levers, he can suspend them in a pleasing mobile configuration, and maybe even sell it for some bread.[35]

So as not to be misled, it is well to think of the behavioral technologies, praxeonomy and mathetics, as *developing technologies* which are merely processes for handling problems associated with education and its subsystems—instructional and learning. Much of the strength of any technological process lies in its ability to identify areas in need of research and in asking the appropriate questions.

In 1969 Paul Saettler said:

. . . It is important . . . to recognize that there are still some basic issues which must be resolved in the behavior sciences before they can be fully applied to the development of a technology of instruction. For example, there is still the question of whether the behavioral sciences are to be a copy of an already outdated Newtonian science or whether they are to grow out of the problems encountered in the study of the learner's choices, purposes or goals. . . .[36]

And Smith and Smith, in *Cybernetic Principles of Learning and Educational Design*, point out a number of inadequacies in reinforcement theory as an adequate explanation of all of human behavior.

Cybernetics

Cybernetics is an emerging science based on "control and communication in the animal and the machine." The term was introduced in its contemporary sense by Wiener in 1947. A paper written in 1943 by Rosenblueth, Wiener, and Bigelow is usually considered the document that laid the groundwork for the modern science.[37]

In a cybernetic sense the human being is regarded as an adaptive control and communication system. For example, the normal human being maintains a body temperature of 98.6°F. But this temperature is not constant within the body; rather, it fluctuates several tenths of a degree to each side of 98.6°. This becomes clear when we think of a person playing a fast game of tennis, perspiring and cooling, and then warming again. Even without this obvious adjustment, the body is constantly making minor changes, either heating or cooling. The body is then seeking to maintain a constant temperature of 98.6° and in this process is continually adapting, based on the feedback it is receiving. This process is referred to as "homeostasis" and is a characteristic of the central aspect of all cybernetic systems. A heating/cooling air-conditioning system governed by a thermostat is an adaptive control system, as is a pressure cooker. It may be generalized that all systems incorporating homeostasis are adaptive systems as they constantly adapt themselves to maintain a present condition in a dynamic environment.

The critical concept in the control aspect of a cybernetic system is that the system is constantly adapting to changing conditions by employing feedback in order to maintain homeostasis.

Communication, the other characteristic of cybernetic systems, is essential for control both within the system and between the system and its environment. Without such communication no input or feedback would be possible.

Karl and Margaret Smith, however, disagree with the use of the term "homeostasis":

> Whatever homeostasis means in physiology, in psychology it means nothing at all. The living, responding organism is designed to respond, to be active rather than inactive, to be dynamic rather than static, to behave constantly until it achieves the pseudo-equilibrium of death.[38]

Instead, they propose a new term, *homeokinetic*, to characterize behavior, "for its organization depends on constant motion generated by the motion systems themselves."[39]

It is strongly urged, if you are interested in pursuing this topic further, that you read Smith's and Smith's, *Cybernetic Principles of Learning and Educational Design*. Also, if you are interested in exploring a new model for science, you may wish to refer to *Beyond Reductionism*, a report on the Alpbach Conference held in 1968. Note: *Beyond Reductionism,* edited by Koestler and Smythies, is published by the Macmillan Company, 866 Third Ave., New York, N.Y. 10022.

Implications of Cybernetic Science for Instruction

Does cybernetic theory help us to answer the questions, What ought to be taught? How? To whom? When? The answer is definitely yes; the field of cybernetics has much to offer. There are three concepts that seem to have particular relevance to the field of instruction:

Concept 1:   The human being is a self-regulating, goal-seeking, adaptive, control, and communication system. The human being learns; that is, he modifies his own patterns of control so that he gains increased control or alters that control by learning. Learning in the human being is the acquisition of new behavior or modification of existing behavior. The individual after learning is not the same person he was before; his repertory has changed and his patterns of control have been altered. In order to structure the environment to maximize the learning for an individual, it is necessary to take into account this altered control through a changed repertory. This implies that the learning, instructional, and educational systems must be adaptive if they are to optimally serve individual learners.

Concept 2:   Smith and Smith draw parallels between the ontogenetic development of an individual and the evolutionary development of the human species.

The overall pattern in both cases is one of increasing control of environment proceeding from gross patterns of control involving dynamic transport and tool-using movements to finer and finer patterns involving manipulative control and symbol systems.

The symbolic tools of thought emerge in roughly the same order in the child and in the human race. Spatial concepts of position, size, and shape precede temporal concepts . . . followed by complicated machine skills and abstract concepts of relationships and interactions.[40]

Historically man's tool-making tradition did more than create technology; it altered man's mechanisms of learning by changing the modes of reaction and the patterns of stimulation in both primary sensorimotor activities and in complex motivated patterns of behavior.[41] . . .Each phase demanded a somewhat different pattern of behavioral control and of learning, but at the same time each extended the learner's ability to control the environment and his relation to it in time and in space. . . . This expansion of feedback control is still going on. In our contemporary technological culture, complex machines and symbol systems provide new means of environmental control and at the same time enhance human understanding of relationships and interactions among environmental events.[42]

To summarize this concept: "Human evolution and history have produced progressive instrumental and symbolic transformations of feedback control of behavior which determine educational design and result in related increases in human intelligence."[43]

It seems to me that this concept should force us to reexamine traditional discipline-oriented curriculum if the learner is to be equipped with the processes necessary to gain ever-increasing control over a dynamic environment.

Concept 3 :   Significant patterns of human learning:
  are determined by the level of development of educational skills and by the design of human symbol systems.[44]
  The cybernetic view of behavior provides a new approach to the study and understanding of educational skills. These skills of speaking, tool-using, drawing, writing, reading, singing, musical instrumentation, numerical manipulation, and controlled observation are closed-loop activities characterized by cybernetic features—that is, generation of productive activity, intrinsic patterns of receptor and sensorimotor organization, feedback control, integration of multi-dimensional response, and instrumental and symbolic transformations of "feedback control."[45]
  Cybernetic theory postulates that precision of response control has increased in human evolution as an aspect of evolving educational design. Man has increased the accuracy, delicacy, and effectiveness of his control systems through the evolution of tools and symbols which systematically enhance his potentialities for closed-loop regulation of adaptive response.[46]
It would seem to be appropriate, based on this concept, to try to increase the level of educational skills within each learner to the highest point possible. This would be done in order to "equip" him with skills in the cybernetic sense described.

To me, these concepts, when synthesized, appear to be the foundation of a new view of instruction and education in general. A view "where education assumes the role of mediator of human progress" and provides man with the skills and process necessary to "escape the space ordered world of his sensory environment into abstractions of scientific and creative thought."[47]

Secondary school pupils today handle concepts and symbol systems that top scientists a few generations ago had not even dreamed of. To do its job effectively, our educational system needs more than teachers and books. It needs all the technological and symbolic machinery that mediates the new knowledge. It needs all the avenues of verbal and nonverbal communication that have been developed. For the machines and techniques of society are more than the fruits of man's knowledge; they are the means of communicating specialized knowledge and skills and the tools for generating new knowledge, skills, techniques, and machines.

Current changes going on in the educational domain sometimes are referred to as a *revolution* in education. Actually, it is not a revolution at all but an inevitable evolution of educational design generated by reciprocal feedback relationships with human, *technological, and social development*. The school and the educational process are not isolated events in the elaboration of man's organized system; they are essential parts of every sector of this development. The elementary school cannot limit itself to the three R's any more than advanced study can be designed completely around a set of great books. Each level of education must adjust to organizational changes and *developments in every facet of human society*. Education must reflect technological as well as communicative changes and social as well as human behavioral changes, if it is to play its role in the progressive evolution of human culture.[48]

Charles F. Jones, vice chairman of the board of Humble Oil and Refining Co., has expressed the need rather well:

We are going to need a change in the very idea and definition of "skill." Instead of being what one has learned, skill will have to become the capacity to learn. Technology has changed so quickly that man must rapidly learn—and unlearn—technical ways that his father did not know and that may well prove useless to his children.

The implications for our educational system are imposing. In many respects, educational practices are simply not geared to produce the new kind of worker.[49]

In order to increase the individual's capability to learn, not only must behavioral science, praxeonomy, and cybernetics be considered, but other organized knowledge must be brought to bear on the problem.

Summary

If there were no additional movements toward the development of a theory of instruction and no further breakthroughs in technology, a decade or more could still be devoted to the application of *presently existing* knowledge and processes to education. Education is beset with the problems and challenges created by a technological society, but we have not employed what is known to the solution of these problems and challenges, through the process of technology.

There are, however, a few indicators that education is beginning to recognize its real problems. The time is now to inventory the available human knowledge that exists, facing the challenge squarely and with a real commitment, to apply applicable scientific and other organized information to the problems confronting education.

A workable theory of instruction, grounded solidly in behavioral principles, has emerged. The ingredients of this theory as outlined in this chapter are found principally in behavioral sciences—the work represented by Thorndike, Skinner, and Gilbert, successively, with certain additions by Premack and Homme, and in cybernetics as represented by Wiener and Smith.

From the reinforcement and operant theory came mathetics and the more comprehensive praxeonomy, and out of the same theories, contingency management. When these developments are synthesized with cybernetic principles, a theory of instruction appears to emerge more complete than any yet developed.

This emergent theory may be stated as follows: The human being is constantly seeking stimulation and modifying his behavior in an effort to control his environment. The direction and character of this modification is determined by his perception of the consequences of that behavior. In order to assist or shape growth in a person, it is necessary to determine his perception of the consequences of any unit, course, curriculum, or other learning experiences. Then through the shaping of these perceptions, so that they more closely approximate reality, the person is able to learn and to make intelligent choices.

3

An Emerging Philosophy and Theory of Curriculum

TOWARD A PHILOSOPHY OF CURRICULUM

Findings in sociology, anthropology, economics, and philosophy must find their way into education in helping to determine the proper content of the curriculum. Rather than approaching specific applications of these disciplines individually, I have chosen to take an interdisciplinary and historical approach.

First, I have explored the state of the art in curriculum, made a historical analysis of scientific approaches to curriculum and instructional development, assessed the state of development of a theory of curriculum; finally, I have attempted to describe what I see as an emerging philosophy of curriculum.

State of the Art

Hilda Taba, a leading curriculum theorist, has said:

When some subjects are selected or retained because they are regarded as a good discipline of the mind, others because of their utility, and still others because they meet the psychological needs of students, the curriculum becomes a hodge-podge.[1]

This is the state of the art. We are in a prescientific era in many areas of curriculum development. To establish the parameters of "curriculum," Taba said:

. . . A curriculum usually contains a statement of aims and of specific objectives; it indicates some selection and organization of content; it either implies or manifests certain patterns of learning and teaching, whether because the objectives demand them or because the content organization requires them. Finally it includes a program of evaluation of the outcomes.[2]

She has said, further, that the difference between curriculum decision-making that follows a scientific method and develops a rational design, and one that does not is that in the former the criteria for decisions are derived from a study of the factors constituting a reasonable basis for the curriculum—the learner, learning process, cultural demands, and content of the disciplines. The curriculum should draw on analyses of society and culture, studies of the learner and the learning process, and analyses of the nature of knowledge.[3]

The rather piecemeal and haphazard development of curriculum occurred in spite of some scientific, sophisticated attempts to make it more systematic and logical, as Taba and others would have it.

A Historical Perspective

A curriculum writer described the current (1918) scene as follows:

. . . We are facing a demand for "specific objectives." Out of this demand there has arisen a new theory of curriculum construction and a new mode of approach. The central theory is simple. Human life, however varied, consists in the performance of specific activities. Education that prepares for life is one that prepares definitely and adequately for these specific activities. However numerous and diverse they may be for any social class, they can be discovered. This requires only that one go out into the world of affairs and discover the particulars of which these affairs consist. These will show the abilities, attitudes, habits, appreciations, and forms of knowledge that men need. These will be the objectives of the curriculum. They will be numerous, definite, and particularized. The curriculum will then be that series of experiences which children and youth must have by way of attaining those objectives.[4]

In order to properly appreciate the development of an adaptive system for deriving curriculum, let's review the developments in the field from the late 1800s to the present.

References to "science" or "a science of education" may be traced to the mid-nineteenth century, but it was not until the 1890s that the scientific movement can be said to have begun. In 1893 the Felkins wrote a book entitled *The Science of Education.*[6] In 1918 Judd wrote his, *The Scientific Study of Education,* and in 1922 posed the following question and then answered it:

Can a substitute for initiative be found in some kind of Systematic procedure that will bring to the door of the school new ideas as fast as these ideas are produced? . . . It is hoped that the net impression produced by the discussion will be one of conviction that there is here a broad field for the exercise of scientific ingenuity.[6]

This scientific movement in curriculum did not take the country by storm; it did not generate even a good breeze. In 1893 the Committee of Ten, like subsequent national committees, focused on the subject matter to be learned, not on the tasks to be performed. Bobbitt, perhaps the greatest proponent of a more pragmatic approach to curriculum construction, published *The Curriculum* in 1918. In this work he laid the foundation for curriculum-building according to scientific principles. He was completely dedicated throughout his life to the construction of a science of education and was perhaps one of the first educational technologists as he attempted to apply scientific principles to the practical problems of education.[7]

ACTIVITY ANALYSIS IN EARLY CURRICULUM CONSTRUCTION

In 1922 Bobbitt, serving as a consultant to the Los Angeles schools, assumed the responsibility for developing and supervising the construction of the curriculum for the junior high school.[8] The steps he followed were outlined in *The Curriculum* as follows: (1) identification of the domains of activity or responsibility in which all children should develop skills; (2) surveying of 2,700 "cultivated and well-trained adults"; (3) identification of 10 major fields of experience, the first nine of which the curriculum of the school should deal with language activities, health activities, citizenship activities, general social activities, spare-time activities, keeping oneself mentally fit, religious activities, parental activities, unspecialized or nonvocational activities, and the labor of one's calling. Tasks were identified within each of these areas. Specific objectives were developed based on the tasks. These specific objectives were stated in terms of performance and formed the measurable basis for what was to be learned by the student.

Simply, then, Bobbitt derived the objectives of the curriculum by finding out what successful and skilled individuals do in life. The difference between this mastery and what the student was able to do constitutes the gap to be reduced through instruction. He saw curriculum development as a three-step procedure:

Step 1: Divide life into major activities.
Step 2. Subdivide each major activity into specific activities through analysis.
Step 3: Translate specific activities to the objectives of education.

Most of Bobbitt's data collection procedures consisted of surveying adults in the community, using questionnaires. The curriculum thus derived was based on the belief that a systematic study of society held greater promise for curriculum development than hunch or speculation and that preparation for life was a fundamental responsibility of education.

The basic questions posed by Bobbitt in his development of the Los Angeles junior high curriculum development to citizens, school officials, and teachers were:

1. Which of the following human characteristics and abilities appear to be generally desirable and therefore legitimate objectives of education?
2. Which ones are frequently, but not generally, desirable?
3. Which ones are probably undesirable and therefore not legitimate objectives of education?
4. Which ones are at least questionable?
5. Which ones should be amended in the statement? What amendment would you suggest?
6. What additional abilities and characteristics, not here suggested, are also desirable, which should be added to the lists by way of completing them? It is for completing an acceptable series of lists that we are particularly anxious to receive suggestions.
7. Which of the following statements of ability are not clear in meaning?[9]

Bobbitt's experience in the Los Angeles project led him to publish *How to Make a Curriculum* in 1924. In this curriculum classic he detailed the philosophy, processes, and procedures of curriculum-derivation, development and implementation. The 19 chapters are divided into three general sections which deal with:

1. The generic problems of curriculum construction, for example, the rationale of and procedures to be employed in formulating educational objectives; the criteria and characteristics of pupil activities.
2. Examples of educational objectives and curriculum experiences in a number of life activity areas.
3. Suggestions to administrators and supervisory personnel.[10]

To Bobbitt, the student was an active organism that needed "unfoldment," a term he uses frequently in his writings—not just a jug to be filled with knowledge or a muscle to be exercised. He believed it necessary to study society on a continuing basis, since it provided the proper substance for curriculum-revision. He wrote and often reiterated that:

> The school is not an agency of social reform. It is not directly concerned with improving society. Its responsibility is to help the growing individual continuously and consistently to hold to the type of human living which is the best practical one for him. This should automatically result in an enormous improvement in society in general. But this improvement is not a thing directly aimed at. It is only a by-product.[11]

In developing curriculum, Bobbitt made use of many people of widely ranging competency, background, and orientation, professionals and laymen alike. "Specialized groups within the community should be held responsible for specially expert services in locating the abilities involved in those portions of the field with which they have to do."[12] He exercised the same principle both in and out of the vocational areas; for example, ". . . physicians and nurses possess specialized ability to assist in formulating the objectives of health education."[13]

The predictable result of this type of philosophy of curriculum development was massive community involvement and effort, with the educator (curriculum specialist) as coordinator. He did not, however, believe that this process could be applied on a state or national scale. It is interesting to note that this was due less to any commitment to local control than to a keen awareness of the problems that he felt would be encountered.

For Bobbitt, education operated on two levels. (1) *the foundational,* which developed the child's potential as a by-product of normal play activity and what he called "unfoldment"; and (2) *the functional,* which related directly and consciously to the tasks that are to be done, those common to all. He felt that the responsibility of the school lay at the second level.[14]

Bobbitt has been criticized for his lack of attention to the "is-ought" problem in formulating educational ends.[15] He thought it rational to employ scientific procedures to "discover" what the ends of education should be. And since society, which provided the subject matter for such study, was changing, the continuous study of society was an important aspect of curriculum development.

He was also criticized by Boyd Bode:

> The method of activity analysis cannot furnish all the material needed for curriculum construction and it cannot furnish guiding principles or objectives.[16]
>
> Activity analysis furnishes no objectives or ideals. It tells us what is, but not what ought to be. . . . Method of activity analysis must be directed by a theory of what education should seek to achieve, and not be regarded as a substitute for such a theory.[17]

OTHER EARLY METHODS OF CURRICULUM CONSTRUCTION

David Snedden and certain other educational sociologists of Bobbitt's time said that the answers to the question, "What shall be the aims of education?" must come from sociology.[18] Their procedure was quite simple:

> Man stands in a two-fold relationship to the world; he is a producer of utilities, and also a consumer; as a producer, he writes books or constructs machines, or produces wheat, or builds houses, or heals the sick, or conveys travelers; and for any of these activities he can be trained. As consumer, however, he is inspired by books, served by machines, nourished by bread, sheltered by houses, healed by physicians, and carried by railways, and for the wise and profitable exercise of these activities he can also be trained.[19]

The Project Method discussed by Charters,[20] McMurry,[21] Kilpatrick,[22] Stevenson,[23] Collins,[24] and others was an attempt to make the school:

. . . continuous with the rest of life. As things are at present, when the child enters the school he is likely to leave his everyday world behind him. He finds himself in an environment that is alien to his interests and purposes. It is for the purpose of remedying this state of affairs that the study of projects is recommended, with the emphasis on "natural setting," "concrete achievement," "worthwhileness," "purposive activity," and "social context."[25]

The roots of the method may be traced to agricultural programs in the secondary school, where, due to lack of resources, a laboratory or growing plots were not available and the student did his experimentation on his father's farm.

Not all projects provided the appropriate challenge or content to make them useful learning experiences. A project had to be selected which would provide a real learning experience:

In a real project the connection between studying and carrying on the job must be sufficiently close so that the job determines directly what is to be studied and gives opportunity to try out the new knowledge from time to time. The studying and the job must proceed abreast.[26]

There are several limitations in the project method as described.
—It does not take into account logical organizations of subject matter or social insight.
—Learning is discontinuous, random, and too immediate in its function unless supplemented.
—Learning is incidental.[27]

Charles McMurry proposed removing the limitation by organizing the subject matter in the manner of the project method.[28]

Bode, commenting on the project method, proposed:

In the interests of our common undertaking it would be better to limit the term project to its original meaning of incidental learning, or else to abstain for a time from talk about the project method and devote ourselves wholeheartedly to a consideration of educational aims, for the purpose of reorganizing our educational materials and methods so as to create new incentives and new meanings for the work of the school.[29]

In all these curriculum methodologies the problem of "what ought to be" was not resolved. John Dewey, the eminent and often misinterpreted educational philosopher and practitioner, interpreted education as "the scientific method by means of which man studies the world, acquires cumulatively knowledge of meanings and values; these outcomes, however, being data for critical study and intelligent living."[30]

CURRICULUM DEVELOPMENT, 1930s TO 1960s

There appear to be three continuing central concerns of curriculum specialists during the 1920s and 1930s:

1. Assuring sound sequence or continuity in the curriculum 2. Establishing consistent relationships between general goals of education and specific objectives that guide teaching 3. Designing curricula that provide a reasonable balance of emphasis among the various areas of study.[31]

The 1940s and 1950s are in need of study, not only for "the development of curriculum proposals and doctrines championed by individuals and organizations, but also for the impact of these proposals on actual educational practices."[32]

The 1950s and into the 1960s were the period of the national curriculum commissions: SMSG (School Mathematics Study Group), BSCS (Biological Sciences Curriculum Study), PSSC (Physical Science Study Committee), CHEM Study, and others.

In summarizing progress in the field of curriculum during the 1960s Goodlad had this to say:

In brief summary, during the past decade significant progress has been made in the precise definition of curricular objectives, in the analysis of ends/means relationships, and in the effective ordering of stimuli for learning. Substantial progress has been made in extending both the understanding of the evaluative process and the use of evaluative data in diagnosing the possible causes of discrepancies between curricular expectancies and curricular accomplishments. In the realm of explaining curricular realities, however, we appear to know little more in 1969 than we knew in 1960. Curricular theory with exploratory and predictive power is virtually non-existent. The most eloquent plea (Schwab, 1969) for correcting this condition directs our attention to the existential character of the curriculum: what it is, how it gets to be the way it is, and how it affects the people who partake of it.[33]

Turning from the process to the content side of educational science, one is struck with the paucity of ordered "findings" from curriculum research—findings in the sense either of scientific conclusions from cumulative inquiry or of tested guidelines for curriculum decisions. There does not seem to be a sizeable community of curriculum scholars who have staked out domains of inquiry with such clarity that successive studies are integrated into a larger whole, gaps identified, and new studies initiated. Nor does there appear to be a companion group of curriculum engineers aware of and drawing upon an established body of professional lore based on research. Schutz's succinct conclusion that "Education appears to be in a prescientific state rather than in a state of scientific revolution" probably applies as much to curriculum as to other subdivisions of education.[34]

RESEARCH FINDINGS

In order to use the information derived from curriculum research, I have categorized general findings under various parts of the "process" applicable to curriculum development, drawn from technology.[35] The vehicle I have employed is the use of direct quotes from various researchers with minimum interference from me.

Performing Task Analyses

The identification and description of competencies for learning has been termed *task analysis*. Ways of conducting a task analysis or the identification of prerequisites are not well established, but empirical and logical strategies are currently being tried (Belcastro, 1961; Gagné and Paradise, 1961; Miller, 1962; Detambel and Stolurow, 1965).[36]

Stating Objectives

Researchers have not demonstrated a workable method by which instructional objectives can reflect objectivity. There is no system for collecting the comprehensive range of facts from which more valid inferences and objectives can be derived. Personal bias and power remain the chief determiners of educational objectives. This is true of the formulation of educational objectives at a national level, at an institutional level within a school system, and at the classroom level where the teacher selects objectives for individual pupils. Two indicators of possible change toward better sampling of pertinent information are (a) The Project TALENT Data Bank (1965) and (b) The National Assessment (McMorris, 1968). Project TALENT provides the first somewhat comprehensive and detailed study of the nation's youth that includes an inventory of their abilities in light of their personal and social needs and the social context in which they live. Similar data about crucial aspects of life now and in the future should also be made systematically available to curriculum planners.[37]

Goodlad identifies two "threads of inquiry" discernible in the field of curriculum:

. . . The formation and use of educational objectives and the systematic arrangement of instructional stimuli.

It is interesting to note that preoccupation with educational objectives has gone through several stages of conceptual and taxonomical analysis into a stage of experimentation. This progression parallels progress in most sciences. That a reaction has begun against the specification of precise, behavioral objectives, and programmed learning sets attests to some maturity in these aspects of curriculum.[38]

In summary, in the past ten years little has been added to knowledge of deriving educational objectives; substantial progress has been made in stating and using educational objectives with precision.[39]

Assessing Student Characteristics

No research findings reported in this area.

Developing Learning Strategies

An examination of the curriculum reform movement in this country during the 1960s reveals that, without exception, those curriculum projects which had the most significant effects upon educational practice produced curriculum materials to implement their new curriculum scheme. To state it bluntly, it takes more than admonitions from curriculum seers, even if they are accompanied by polished curriculum guides, to alter the procedures of busy educational practitioners.[40]

The broadest interpretation of the phrase "curriculum materials" includes such educational devices as textbooks, audiovisual equipment, and bulletin board displays. However, because rigorous research regarding curricular materials will normally be focused on those materials as some form of treatment variable, it seems appropriate to consider only those curriculum materials which are essentially *replicable,* i.e., materials which permit repeated investigations of their attributes and effects.[41]

The research gaps Popham identifies in developing learning strategies are:

First, studies of the revision process to improve the quality of curriculum materials have not been frequently conducted. There seems to be an overriding faith in the idea that materials revised to be consistent with empirical tryout data will become better, but this has not been clearly demonstrated. Certainly the manner in which revisions can be made most efficiently has not been carefully treated.

Although there are some investigators who are beginning to study ways of evaluating the quality of curriculum materials with diverse kinds of measures (measures which deal with noncognitive as well as the more common kinds of cognitive learner outcomes), there is a great need for research on newer evaluative techniques. Can affective measures be devised to reliably assess the learner's approach tendencies toward particular kinds of curriculum materials? How can researchers determine the degree to which the learner will remain "plugged in" to the materials as he goes through them? Mager's text (1968) about measurement and instructional strategies related to learner interest is relevant. Evaluative research which attempts to study other than standard types of measurement strategies definitely needs to be conducted.

[Popham calls for] more studies . . . that possess clear relevance to the practical decisions which must be made regarding preparation of curriculum materials. . . . Curriculum materials may provide one of the most formidable change agents for modifying educational practice. To the extent that this is true, educational researchers obviously need to devote more systematic attention to this area of research than they previously have.[42]

Validation-Evaluation

At present, formative evaluation methods have much the same status as the invisible needle and thread used by the tailors in the "Emperor's

New Clothes." (Schutz, 1968) Pointing out that formative evaluation efforts have been highly content-oriented, Schutz advocated shifting to a product orientation in which the criteria for gauging instructional improvement become straightforward and the application of formative evaluation procedures become more meaningful.[43]

Schutz described a "primitive" model for product development research. This model may be described as two approaches involving a convergent methodology. The first is a trial revision cycle working within the boundaries of the present instructional system to create a product that will achieve predetermined objectives now! The second approach is a follow-up and introduces modifications in one or more of the major dimensions of practice, e.g., use of a computer-based instructional management system.[44]

Curriculum developers have tended to assume an isomorphism between their interpretation of curriculum guides and instructional materials and that of teachers and students. As long as their assumption was not questioned, a gentlemen's agreement held. However, word is leaking out that a number of cherished curriculum beliefs are figments of the researcher's theoretical imagination. The nongraded classroom appears to be indistinguishable from teacher-instruction in schools, and endemic gaps are being identified "between emotionally-toned accounts of the ideology and the day-to-day reality in the life of innovative schools and classrooms" (Smith and Deith, 1968, p. 5). An overarching methodological issue is the invention of means to separate credibility from dependability. Gap-creating work appears to be necessary for separating advertising from data; and gap-filling work seems essential for separating conjectural from functional relationships involving educational phenomena.[45]

Evaluation must be designed to determine the relationship not only between stated goals and the degree of their attainment but also between an initial conception of the practice designed to achieve them and the practice actually developed. Such diagnostic information is definitely more helpful than knowledge about attainment of objectives alone.[46]

One application taking cognizance of this need is the Discrepancy Evaluation Model being used in Pittsburgh, Pennsylvania (Provus, 1969).

Unfortunately, the major components of a causal model of learning, let alone the respective contribution of each component, are unknown. How much of the whole do we assign to family context, to teachers, to the curriculum? The answers will be a long time in coming. . . . reviews of research suggest that the curriculum field is not very advanced in the conceptualizing and theory-building needed to find the answers. The trees are receiving increasingly systematic attention, but it is difficult to know whether analysis of them will add up to a better understanding of the forest.[47]

It is encouraging to note the new emphasis on experimental work *within* the field of curriculum. By manipulating variables in school practice and noting the consequences, curriculum knowledge is gained, and at the same time the objectives, content, and methods of instruction are changed. As long as studies in curriculum were descriptive and analytical, it was difficult for curricular knowledge to be a force in shaping what was taught and how it was taught.[48]

FINDINGS

Just what does all this research in curriculum and instruction point to? The following list should be a start:

1. Most students can master what is taught to them.
2. The task of the instructor is to find ways to enable students to master the subject.
3. Given enough time, nearly all students can attain mastery.
4. The learner must understand the nature of the task he is to learn and the procedure he is to follow in learning it.
5. It may be profitable to provide alternative learning opportunities.
6. The teacher should provide feedback on the learner's particular errors and difficulties.
7. Frequent feedback to the learners and specific instruction is effective in helping the learner to achieve.
8. The teacher must find ways to alter the time individuals need for learning.
9. Formulation of specific objectives of the learning task is an important precondition of mastery.
10. It is useful to break a course or subject into small units of learning and to test at the end of each unit.
11. Student effort is increased when small groups of two or three students meet regularly for as long as an hour to review their test results and to help one another overcome the difficulties identified by means of the test.[49]

Perhaps the most encouraging conclusion drawn was:
Curriculum is becoming more rational because researchers and practitioners are beginning to realize that the desired changes in the learner are the true "ends" and that methods and instructional sequences used

to produce those changes are the "means," not to be prized but appraised.[50]

TOWARD A PHILOSOPHY, THEORY, AND PRACTICE OF CURRICULUM DEVELOPMENT

It is obvious that comprehensive answers have still not been found, or even seriously sought in some cases, to the basic questions Bobbitt sought to answer in the 1920s:

What should be taught?
How should we derive what is to be taught?
How should we keep it current?
How do we know if the student has learned?
And is the learning of any practical use to him?

It appears that current commentators on the educational scene aren't saying anything really new but sadly are still accurate: "Present techniques of investigation are wrong, and as a result there is almost no pertinent information about how well ideas acquired in school are used several years later."[51]

Goodlad (1968) and Schwab (1969) call for studies of curriculum, "the way it is," and for the development of a "curriculum theory with truly useful explanatory and predictive power."

We simply do not know very much about the way it is at any level (social, institutional, or instructional) of curriculum development or decision-making. Curriculum researchers have not identified the gates through which ideas pass nor what happens to them on the way to the classroom; how those carefully developed materials are used or if they are used at all; how conflicts between the ideological curriculum of materials and the mental curriculum of teachers are reconciled; what reaches and attracts the student and what does not; and on and on. There is no doubt about the need for better curriculum experiments . . . but paralleling these must be equally well but differently designed studies seeking to explain the nature of what reasonably can be called "the curriculum," what affects its formulation, and what it affects and how.[52]

As has been noted by Taba and others, there is no comprehensive theory of curriculum development. This seems to be due to a multiplicity of reasons:

> ... not the least of which is a lack of clarity and outright conflicts in the basic sciences from which education draws its data and guiding principles. Conflicts ... in philosophical and psychological theories regarding the nature of the individual, the nature of learning, the goals of our culture and the role of the individual in that culture.[53]

Society and Culture in Curriculum

Bruner has suggested that the final basis for redefining education must be the changing society:

> It may well be the case that not only are we entering a period of technological maturity in which education will require constant redefinition, but that the period ahead may involve such a rapid rate of change in specific technology that narrow skills will become obsolete within a reasonably short time after their acquisition. Indeed, perhaps one of the defining properties of a highly matured technology is that there exists a lively likelihood of major technological change within the compass of a single generation—just as ours has seen several such major changes.[54]
>
> It would seem, indeed, as if the principal thing about tools and techniques is that they beget other more advanced ones at ever-increasing speed. And as the technology matures in this way, education in its very nature takes on an increasing role by providing the skills needed to manage and control the expanding enterprise.[55]

Bruner then cautions us that the first response of educational systems in this situation is to produce technicians, engineers, and scientists as needed, but to neglect the management of the enterprise.[56]

Smith and Smith have said:

> The main challenge in the science of human learning is to understand the requirements of educational design at all levels, that is, in providing feedback control to initiate learning, in designing tools and symbolic processes to integrate individual development with social-cultural evolution, and in simulating human organization to provide specialized pragmatic experience. The challenge of education is to maintain its role

as the mediator of human progress. Education must keep pace with intellectual and technological change, for it is the means of conserving and consolidating such change. Only by passing on his educational skills can man escape the space-ordered world of his sensory environment into the abstractions of scientific and creative thought.[57]

Hilda Taba has outlined for us certain characteristics of our society and their implications for curriculum.

Knowledge and learning need to be so selected and organized that they will provide a young adult with a sense of unity, of meaningful relationship between himself and his world.[58]

Another task seems to be to create minds which can cope with the problems of living in a rapidly changing world.[59]

A society which lives by specialization requires an education which can create a balanced overall curriculum and a perspective toward the whole culture and whole man.[60]

She has emphasized on numerous occasions the necessity for the school to develop a value orientation in the learner. But to me, her most poignant plea is for a developing in the learner of interpersonal dynamic "techniques that can produce consensus out of disagreement, and common purposes out of conflict of values."[61] These techniques have not been completely discovered, and her call includes their development.

The study of culture is another source from which may be drawn certain curricular notions. Bruner has said:

A culture in its very nature is a set of values, skills, and ways of life that no one member of the society masters. . . . Knowledge in this sense is like a rope, each strand of which extends no more than a few inches along its length, all being intertwined to give a solidarity to the whole. The conduct of our educational system has been curiously blind to this interdependent nature of knowledge.[62]

Culture as interpreted by anthropologists is a fertile source of data on curriculum:

. . . Anthropological concepts have a special relevance to education, and what anthropologists say about culture—its characteristics and problems—is of unique importance to the development of criteria for curriculum-making.[63]

There is substantial evidence to support the contention that neither study of society or culture have truly influenced curriculum: "In spite of long-standing verbal iteration of the importance of analysis of culture and of social needs, this analysis has never cut deeply into practical curriculum-making."[64]

What Does It All Mean? Three Implications

What sort of guidance may be derived from the foregoing examination of the field of curriculum that will assist us in developing an instructional model?

The application of scientific method to the field of curriculum has a long historical tradition as such things go in the field of education. Bobbitt left us a legacy of procedures in curriculum-making that lacked only a solid philosophical base. Many of the more recent curriculum movements clearly illuminate a number of blind alleys in curriculum-construction. It is safe to say that more has been learned about what *not to do*, than *what to do* in building a curriculum. Several prominent figures in education, including Goodlad and Taba, have said that we are in prescientific era in curriculum as in other realms of education.

A number of creative individuals, anthropologists, sociologists, and others are beginning to draw implications for curriculum from studies of society and culture.

Perhaps the *prime* implication that may be drawn from studies of curriculum is that a working philosophy is necessary. A *second* implication is that whatever philosophy is derived, the resulting curriculum-development process must be based in technology, so that findings from the basic science may be drawn upon. A *third* implication is that the philosophy derived must both reflect and lead the society in which it is based. Let's return to the basic question that must be answered by curriculum to see if we can now better answer it.

What Ought to Be Taught?

A major problem in instruction today is determining what is to be taught, or less obviously but more important, what is to be learned by the student. This determination of curriculum must be empirically based, which means the original specification and ongoing curricular modification must be based on what the student "needs to know," "needs to be able to do," and more controversially, "needs to feel."

Based on conclusions drawn from this chapter, it appears that a challenge is presented for modifications of existing techniques of deriving curriculum. It is apparent that curriculum, developed in one case because it is discipline for the mind or has life utility value, and in another because it meets the life needs of students, results in what Dr. Taba called a "hodgepodge."

Is curriculum to be derived from the disciplines, or from an analysis of manpower requirements in the community? From an analysis of the social and cultural needs of society, or from the human needs of the potential consumers—the students? Of these, how will they be derived? From the occupational needs of the community or from the occupational needs of the individual? If both, which is paramount?

Education should be concerned with the *how* of learning; the *what* and *why* are properly the province of society. It is not the responsibility of the educator, nor should it be, to determine what man is to be. That is the responsibility of all of us. It is the purpose of education to equip the individual with the tools, skills, knowledge, and models for formulation of a value system that will allow him to become the whole man—the individual able to lead the "good life," to seek full humanity. Education should serve to increase the alternatives, lift the horizons, and make it possible for the individual to "do his own thing" rather than "no-thing."

What, then, is the proper content of education? What is to be learned, if education is to provide man with the tools and disposition to enable him to strive toward increasing humanity? What are the tools, procedures, and attitudes that will make it possible for each person to develop his greatest potential as a human being? The individual simply must *learn how to learn efficiently*—this is the answer to "what ought to be taught."

LEARNING HOW TO LEARN EFFICIENTLY

What does learning consist of? Learning is the modification of behavior, and consists of an individual responding to stimuli in ever more satisfying ways. The vehicle of the learning process is communications— the receipt, decoding, processing, encoding, transmitting, receiving, etc., of messages. The principal skills in this process are *decoding* and *encoding*. Cybernetically speaking, the human being is a self-regulating, goal-seeking, adaptive (feedback-regulated), control and communication system.

Stimuli emanating from the environment are in some kind of coded form and carry no meaning in and of themselves; they become meaningful only as they are decoded and perceived by the receiver. The meaning of the message resides with the receiver.

Messages may be transmitted and received through one or a combination of senses. At times, conflicting messages are transmitted simultaneously; since the meaning of the message rests with the perceptions of the receiver, this may be quite unknown to the sender. A typical example of this phenomenon is the college professor lecturing about the latest teaching methodology and the student decoding his message as, "What you do speaks so loudly, I can't hear what you're saying."

The person who wants to get his ideas across to someone else who wants to communicate must encode his messages in such a way that when received by another person they convey the intended meaning.

It is now possible through technology to communicate almost without constraint of time or place. The symbolic systems employed are becoming increasingly complex as communication requirements grew at a geometric rate. It is possible to communicate man to man, man to machine, machine to machine, or even commune with nature in self-satisfying ways over great distances of space and time.

I see these decoding and encoding skills as the basic skills and the communications process as the principal process of learning. Wiener casts some additional light on this concept:

> It apparently is built into the brain itself, that we are to have a preoccupation with codes and with the sounds of speech, and that the preoccupation with codes can be extended from those dealing with speed to those that concern themselves with visual stimuli.[65]
>
> . . . The human interest in language seems to be an innate interest in coding and decoding. . . .[66]

These basic skills are not fixed skills, nor is the problem a static one. In order to reveal the essence of concept, we must keep in mind the cybernetic nature of the problem and the natural state of organisms, including man. As Wiener has said:

> To describe an organism, we do not try to specify each molecule in it, and catalogue it bit by bit, but rather to answer certain questions about it which reveal its pattern: a pattern which is more significant and less probable as the organism becomes, so to speak, more fully an organism.[67]

The heart of cybernetics lies in man as an organic system:

> We are not whirlpools in a river of ever-flowing water. We are not stuff that abides, but patterns that perpetuate themselves.[68]

What do we know about people which when coupled with these ideas will help us in describing a theory of curriculum development? I see three areas:

1. Since learning is a modification of behavior and the human being is a behavior acquiring organism, man's natural state is learning.
2. The behavior-acquisition process may be optimized by providing opportunity for increasing the range of encoding and decoding skills in the learner, thus providing him with the capability of processing increasingly complex stimuli in a meaningful (self-satisfying) manner.
3. Our aim with each student is to help him reach the point where his encoding and decoding skills are self-satisfying and which permit him to acquire other encoding and decoding skills efficiently on his own. When this point of self-satisfaction is reached, we have what has traditionally been referred to as a self-actuating learner.

The human being is under a constant bombardment of stimuli from the environment, so he must learn to be selective in his attention to competing stimuli. If the task of education is to increase the learner's decoding capabilities to the point of his own self-satisfaction, then the contents of the messages employed will be based primarily on the motivational characteristics of the individual learner. For example, where a learner needs to be able to interpret verbal symbols in the form of printed words at a basic level, it really makes little difference whether the student exercises this decoding skill through "Dick and Jane" or a low-vocabulary *Catcher in the Rye*.

A higher-level decoding task may involve the decoding of phrases with subtleties of meaning requiring attention to very complex stimuli; on this account, they may not provide as much range of alternative content. Still, for the most part, the content will be dictated by the motivational characteristics of the individual learner, that is, what turns him on and off and what interests him. Therefore, the individualization of instruction occurs in this area of content and in pacing—that is, the rate of learner movement through the learning sequence.

Wiener has illustrated a second major step in the processing of information beyond initial reception and decoding:

Semantically significant information from the cybernetic point of view is that which gets through the line-plus-filter, rather than that which gets through the line alone. In other words, when I hear a passage of music, the greater part of the sound gets to my sense organs and reaches my brain. However, if I lack the perception and training necessary for the aesthetic understanding of musical structure, this information will meet a block, whereas if I were a trained musician it would meet an interpreting structure or organization which would exhibit the pattern in a significant form which can lead to aesthetic appreciation and further understanding.[69]

In essence, the learner, by having decoding and encoding skills in his repertoire, will be equipped with the tools necessary to acquire whatever skills, knowledges, and attitudes become necessary to him during his lifetime. Lower level skills, because of the control-seeking nature of the learner, will beget ever more complex skills. These decoding and encoding processes, empirically derived, are structured in hierarchical format from simple to complex for each successive stimulus configuration, hence each decoding and encoding problem becomes more complex.

The major thrust of curriculum-development should be to determine the types of encoding and decoding processes necessary to life now, with a look toward the future. To me, this seems the most viable alternative in view of the nature of the learning process, the dynamic quality of society, and the basic state of the human organism—behavior modification.

Summary

Let's return to the questions posed earlier in this chapter, in order to answer the basic question: "What ought to be taught?" or the more appropriate question, "What does the student need to know and need to be able to do?"

The student needs to know and be able to do whatever is necessary to enable him to learn efficiently the myriad knowledges, skills, processes, and attitudes that will lead him to realize his full humanity in a dynamic environment, through the utilization of the tools and technology available to and/or created by him. He must be able to manipulate increasingly complex symbolic systems. The skills for decoding and encoding ever more complex stimuli are partially known today and the remainder need to be derived empirically. Just as the "proper study of mankind is man," the proper study of the communications process and the skills comprising it is observation of it in a "real world" setting.

The source of these decoding and encoding skills necessary to meet life's requirements is the community. For example:

1. What sort of decoding skills are necessary to be a "functional citizen" of the community today? What skills equip the learner with the skills to learn how to manipulate the increasingly complex symbolic systems he will encounter a decade from now, or 50 or more years from now?
2. What decoding and encoding skills are necessary in order to appreciate literature, art, drama, music?
3. What decoding and encoding skills are required in order to learn how to maintain one's health and use leisure time in a self-fulfilling manner?
4. What encoding and decoding skills are necessary to acquire an understanding of one's self, his society, and the relationship of self to society?
5. What encoding and decoding skills are necessary to enable the individual to efficiently utilize tools and the process of technology to solve the problems facing mankind, including the very problems created by such technology?

Through broad exposure to a wide range of these skills in real problem-solving situations, the student will come to exercise his expanded repertoire in ever-ascending and self-satisfying ways.

In many ways our present discipline-oriented methodologies for deriving curriculum might be condemned, much as Wiener condemned certain organizations:

Those who would organize us according to permanent individual functions and permanent individual restrictions condemn the human race to move at much less than half-steam. They throw away nearly all our human possibilities and by limiting the modes in which we may adapt ourselves to future contingencies, they reduce our chances for a reasonably long existence on this earth.[70]

Perhaps the most poignant plea for curriculum development was made by Rosenblith:

Our adjustment to the world around us depends upon the informational windows that our senses provide. Our culture depends upon the relevant use of the vast stores of information that we have accumulated, and in a real sense access to specialized information is a form of feedback that may be equivalent to the advantages of economic, political, or military power.[71]

As Wiener has said: "Feedback is a method of controlling a system by reinserting into it the results of its past performances." All curricula must stand the empirical test of usefulness in the real world, based on this feedback. Therefore that which does not measure up will be refined or discarded and replaced with other skills and processes. Through this process community college education may gain even more relevant curriculum by formulating better answers to the age-old question of what should be taught. The "saber-toothed curriculum" of Benjamin may perhaps finally recede never to return.

4

A Philosophy Emerges

However the answer to the question, "what ought to be taught," is eventually derived, it must be based on a philosophy of education, a philosophy consistent with the democratic ideals of our society. "A philosophy of education, like any theory, has to be stated in words, in symbols. But so far it is more than verbal; it is a plan for conducting education. Like any plan, it must be framed with reference to what is to be done and how it is to be done."[1] Any such philosophy, to be grounded in democratic ideals, must:

1. Place the individual at the center of the system.
2. Prepare the individual to flourish in a dynamic society that requires constant modifications of his behavior.
3. *Not* impose the standards of the present society on any future generation. (As Bode said: "Sound education does not seek to prescribe belief or conduct, but to provide for the creation of new standards in accordance with new conditions and new needs."[2] And as Bode later said: "Each generation must define afresh the nature, direction, and aims of education to assure such freedom and rationality as can be attained for a future generation."[3]
4. Recognize the individual as an idiosyncratic learner who modifies his behavior based on his perceptions of the consequences.
5. Prepare and equip the individual for freedom.
6. Develop the inborn capacity to love in each individual.

CONCLUSIONS

When I synthesize the data and ideas from instruction and curriculum with the basic philosophical notions above, I come to the following conclusions, which I find useful as a basis for developing an educational program:

1. There is substantial evidence that technology will not dehumanize man. In fact, there is evidence that man is "dependent upon tools and technology for his very humanity."[4]
2. Man must utilize the process of technology to solve the increasingly complex problems, many of which are created by the very process that will solve them.
3. Education, in seeking the status of an applied science, must develop lines of communication with the basic sciences so that present knowledge and new findings may be applied to the problems of education through the employment of the technological process.

In applying these conclusions to curriculum and instruction, it becomes imperative that: (1) curriculum grow out of a philosophy of education that is consistent with the ideals of our society and that it stand the empirical test of usefulness to the individual and in life in general, and (2) we base instruction in the emerging theory of instruction that has grown out of what we know about how people learn. It must also stand the empirical test of efficiency in producing learning in each individual.

The task of instruction is to:

1. Specify the outcomes in terms of the learner's behavior.
2. Determine what the individual learner perceives as the consequences of the behavior.
3. Shape his perceptions of these consequences to more nearly approximate reality.
4. Provide learning experiences that will increase the encoding and decoding skill levels of the learner, thereby permitting him to employ increasingly complex symbolic systems. These skills will enable him to efficiently acquire ever more fulfilling behavior consistent with the stated philosophy.
5. Provide checks to determine that the learner is becoming more efficient and effective as a learner and modify experiences as necessary based on this feedback.

5

An Instructional Systems Model

This chapter deals historically with the systems approach as applied to instruction; the identification of models presently applied to instruction, with a brief description of each; and the development of a preliminary instructional systems model, synthesized from the existing models.

The application of a systems approach to instruction has been variously described as "common sense by design,"[1] a logical process of analysis and synthesis, and as the application of "Anasynthesis." *Anasynthesis* is a process consisting of four major parts: analysis, synthesis, modeling, and simulation. These often follow in sequential order. *Analysis* is performed on existing information, *synthesis* is performed to create a new whole, *models* are constructed to predict effectiveness without the actual implementation of the system, *simulation* is performed to reveal alternative solutions.[2]

The following narrative is exemplary of a systems approach, perhaps in its most basic form. It is a description of an early project conducted by the System Development Corporation:

In 1958, we started a project to explore programmed-instruction technology. It appeared that existing programs provided for individual differences in rate of learning but did not provide for differences in the level of component skills of students during the course of instruction. A computer-based teaching machine was developed to provide for such individual differences. Students doing well would skip instructional segments while those having difficulty on a particular concept would be branched to remedial segments necessary to successful performance on the concept. Experience with this machine quickly revealed that its effect on learning depended mostly on the effectiveness of the instructional materials used by the machine. One study effort, in an attempt to design improved instructional materials, surveyed the research literature on learning and made a series of experimental comparisons. The most notable result of the formal hypothesis-testing activities was that no statistically significant differences among experimental treatments were obtained. Different sequencing procedures, cueing techniques, response modes, display formats, and reinforcement procedures had but limited effect. Variables suggested by different learning theories were manipulated but again with little practical impact on student learning. The formal hypothesis testing and the literature search were abandoned and popular, new, commercially produced, programmed instructional material was tried. Considerable publicity had been given this material as the latest in modern instructional technology. It also failed to produce its advertised objectives.

Finally a procedure was tried that did succeed. This consisted of a careful specification of learning objectives in behavioral and measurable form, followed by a succession of evaluation-revision cycles. Each defect in the instructional material was detected, the behavioral components involved were reanalyzed, and specific changes were made in the defective segment. Ideas for possible changes were obtained from interviews and individual tutorial sessions with students. Repeated evaluation-revision cycles were conducted until new students exposed to the materials consistently achieved the desired objectives. Thus the developing package of materials was continually improved in the direction of a given set of absolute objectives.

This technique is quite different from a one-time evaluative comparison of the first version of the new package with "conventional" procedures ("conventional" is that used by the other school). The evaluation-revision cycle is more like the engineering process, where the development activity is followed through to the final stage of implementation, and is much more costly in time and effort than the one-shot comparative study. However, the engineering approach, which begins with system objectives and uses self-correction procedures, culminates in workable tools and procedures that are guaranteed to do certain specified things for the instructor, while the traditional comparative-assessment study seldom goes further than a research report having little impact on a classroom practice. The engineering approach implies a commitment to make a new product or procedure work, rather than merely making a single evaluation for the purpose of deciding whether or not to adopt it—almost all new developments fail on the first try.[3]

C. R. Carpenter describes the same process differently:

> A system design for an educational enterprise would provide: a conceptual framework for planning, orderly consideration of functions and resources including personnel and technical facilities . . ., the kinds and amount of resources needed, and a phased and ordered sequence of events leading to the accomplishment of specified and operationally defined achievements. A systems approach should provide a way of checking on the relation of performances of all components to factors of economy and should reveal any inadequacies of the several components, including the faults of timing and consequently of the entire system.[4]

The principal features of the systems approach are described by the National Commission on Technology, Automation and Economic Progress in these words:

> The [system] approach has two main features. First, objectives are stated clearly in performance terms rather than in particular technologies or pre-existing models. . . . The advantage of specifying objectives in system terms is that it forces decision makers to so delineate the factors that a rational comparison of alternative solutions is possible.
>
> The second feature of the system approach is its emphasis on the interrelations within a system. The usual approach has been to divide a problem into more manageable subproblems. . . . Since any one problem is so directly linked with others, it has to be viewed in its entirety. In short, what a system approach implies is comprehensive planning so that we can trace out the effects, progressive and regressive, of any set of choices and decisions upon all other relevant decisions.[5]

The systems approach is nothing more than a procedure by which certain types of problems may be processed. It is a procedure characterized by certain essential elements:

1. A clear description of goals and objectives.
2. A clear delineation of constraints.
3. The establishment of measures of effectiveness.
4. The synthesis of alternate solutions which consider all significant aspects of the problem.
5. The establishment of cost elements.
6. A cost-effectiveness analysis to establish trade-offs among solutions.
7. The continuing evaluation and feedback.[6]

In the final analysis, most system designers appear to agree with Banathy: "The key criterion by which the effectiveness or adequacy of the performance of a system can be evaluated is how closely the output of the system satisfies the purpose for which it exists."[7]

In applying the systems approach to instruction there seems to be confusion in the minds of educators as to just what this approach is. As I reviewed so-called instructional systems models it became apparent that many persons were thinking of an instructional methodology like the audio-tutorial approach or lecture method, rather than a carefully designed procedure for processing the problems of instruction.

HISTORICAL DEVELOPMENT OF A SYSTEMS APPROACH TO INSTRUCTION

Threads of systems-thinking may be traced throughout most of recorded history. Dr. Leonard Silvern, perhaps the "father of systems-thinking in education" and the leading chronicle of the history of the "systems approach," gives Herbart the distinction of being the originator or "great grandfather" of the instructional systems movement. Silvern defines the "systems approach" as the process of anasynthesis:

> *Anasynthesis* is a process consisting of four major parts: analysis, synthesis, modeling, and simulation. These often follow in sequential order: *analysis* is performed on existing information, *synthesis* is performed to create a new whole, *models* are constructed to predict effectiveness without the actual implementation of the system, *simulation* is performed to reveal alternative solutions.[8]

Herbart and his mentor Leibnitz understood and utilized the basic process of analysis and synthesis, developed a mathematical model applicable to human behavior, worked out the "formal steps"—*clearness, association, system,* and *method,* and in the words of Silvern: "His [Herbart's] understanding in the early 1800s of Analysis and Synthesis in referring to system transcends the presentday awareness of most educators in the U.S.!"[9]

If Herbart is thought of as the great grandfather of the "systems approach," then Charters might well be described as the grandfather. In 1923 he published perhaps his greatest work, *Curriculum Construction,* a synthesis of the preceding contributions by men such as Herbart, Ziller, Rein, Mulliner, DeGarmo, and McMurry. Allen, a leading innovator in "vocational" education of the day, had ideas in job analysis that strongly influenced Charters. Interestingly, in many ways Allen was far more influential in his area than was Charters in general education. His plea was for a curriculum that was pragmatic, as well as for instruction based on job analyses that detail behaviors transferable to the real world.[10]

Charters may be said to have laid the foundation for the field of educational engineering. Two of his later papers were "Is There a Field of Educational Engineering?" (1945) and "The Era of the Educational Engineer" (1951). His last published thoughts, according to Silvern,[11] may have been:

> I predict a change in the emphasis in the next half-century in the field of education. The shift will be from the exploration of ideas and concepts to the development of techniques for putting them into practice. The five methods used by the educational engineer will continue to be used to identify the idea to be worked on . . . analyze it . . . build a structure . . . a curricular unit . . . an operational technique . . . an instructional method . . . operate the tool and try it out in practice . . . test the results to measure the efficiency and practicality of what he has constructed. . . .[12]

Charters' words of the 1940s and 1950s have reverberated up and down the halls of academia and even in Congress, but in spite of the crises facing education and the nation, the task he set nearly 20 years ago remains largely unrealized:[13] "I predict concerted national action in the field of educational engineering. The task of building an efficient body of methods in usable form cannot be left to individual initiative."[14] The front is not quiet, there are those who are still stumping for a national effort in developing a technology of education:[15]

> It is vital to reassess the role and functions of education and establish a "new education." The new education must be a science; not necessarily a theoretical science, but at least an "applied science" based on empirical processes.[16]

Charters made another prediction which is still awaiting complete fulfillment:

> Research laboratories will expand their geographical areas to include the schools of the nation, because good engineering techniques demand that methods developed in the laboratory be tried out in practice before

their validity is demonstrated and prior to their release for general use. . . .[17]

World War II produced, in addition to many complex problems, a group of human beings who thought scientifically. They were inquisitive, supporting no sacred cows without empirical data to support their existence. They were objective; they valued and thrived on a process of investigation committed to discovering cause and effect. They respected empirical results that could stand the test of reproducibility. Unfortunately, these men were not to be found within the field of education beyond a stray maverick now and then. In 1951 one such maverick said: ". . . selection of what to teach obviously depends upon what the learners are to do with the skill or knowledge acquired. . . .[18] With his customary eloquence, Silvern got right to the heart of the problem: "Remember—a fire cannot be extinguished with a training certificate. . . ."[19]

D. Wolfle, a strong proponent of job analysis, sought to move the state of the art forward. He was also concerned, as were others, about the problem of training obsolescence—skills that were critical one month became, because of new techniques or other reasons, obsolete the next. He felt training had to keep pace.[20] Wolfle further saw as necessary, ". . . a different kind of job analysis, one that describes the task in terms of its psychological components instead of in terms of its work units. . . ."[21]

Another related area of concern was implementation of the concept of internal and external criteria. A man could be trained to "lead" a pipe joint, and while in training demonstrate this skill to the predetermined standard of excellence. On the job, however, he might find that the cast iron pipe requiring "leaded" joints had been replaced with copper which required a different process, one that he had not been trained to perform. Clearly, then, both internal and external criteria need to be assessed and the information fed back into the system in such a way as to insure modification as necessary on a continuing basis.

Silvern credits Swain (1954) with developing one of the earliest post-World War II flowcharts to focus on the trainee-instructor relationship.[22]

In the 1940s a two-line statement appeared at the bottom of a wallet-sized card as a part of "Training Within Industry Programs" of the War Manpower Commission. It read:

IF THE WORKER HASN'T LEARNED
THE INSTRUCTOR HASN'T TAUGHT[32]

This must certainly be one of the earlier statements of accountability in training and education.

The beginning of the era in which systems started to be at least mentioned in connection with all aspects of instruction may be traced back to 1957 when Silvern spoke of the "integrated training program," a term he used synonomously with "system."

> ... Since the *total* training program must serve the needs of the job, this program in a relatively short time will have the technical skills and knowledge problems of the job *feed back* through the "work experience" phase into the *total* training program. In this way, the curriculum will be continually modified to meet occupational needs. In the same manner, the interaction of work training experience will call for the modification of occupational concepts, procedures and policies to make *both* the job and the training program dynamic, progressive entities. *It is this interaction which forms the basic* philosophy of training program integration. . . .[24]

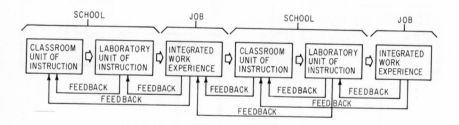

Figure 5-1. Flow Chart Illustrating School-Job Relationship with
Feedback. (From Silvern, *Systems Engineering*, p. 46.)

Silvern said of the "breakthroughs" in the 1950s:

Isn't there a familiar ring of the 1920's and 30's to the "discoveries" of the 1950's? Isn't it odd that job analysis had to be invented all over again, that ANALYSIS and SYNTHESIS had to be rediscovered, that only the names, dates, faces, and words seem different but the basic staff . . . the fundamental elements . . . are exactly the same . . . only the systems had become *more* complex?[25]

In 1960 Riley and Riley, in a model of a social system, explored several essential ideas, including the concept of interdependency:

> Thus any slight disturbance introduced into the system will have ramifications throughout the whole and will be counteracted by various reactions tending to restore a state of equilibrium. This means that any contemplated innovation must be viewed as potentially affected by, and in turn affecting, all the other parts of the system. . . .[26]

In 1960 Pask detailed the interface between student and machine in an instructional setting.[27]

Stolurow (1961) charted an adaptive teaching machine system where feedback was employed to modify the program.[28]

Forrester, a professor of industrial management at the Massachusetts Institute of Technology in 1957, developed "Industrial Dynamics," an application of electrical engineering systems concepts to the problems of

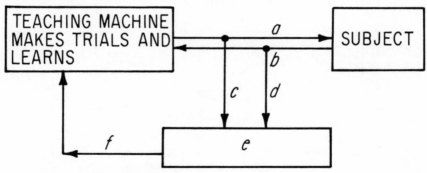

a Teaching machine moves
b Subject response moves
c, d Input to score
e Scoring device
f Output from scoring device gives permission to learn only if score is highly valued

Figure 5-2.   Flow Chart Illustrating Student-Machine-Score Relationship. (From Pask, "Adaptive Teaching," p. 362.)

management and economics. He may also be a chronicler of what is to come, since in 1964 he said:

. . . The next two decades may well be a period of transition from the era when society has focused its pioneering attention on science to the era in which we will turn priority attention to understanding the dynamic behavior of our social problems . . . what does technical engineering bring to enterprise engineering?
  Five contributions seem conspicuous:
  1. the concept of designing a system
  2. the principles of feedback control
  3. the clear distinction between policy making and decision making
  4. the low cost of electronic communication and logic
  5. the substitution of simulation for analytic solutions.[29]

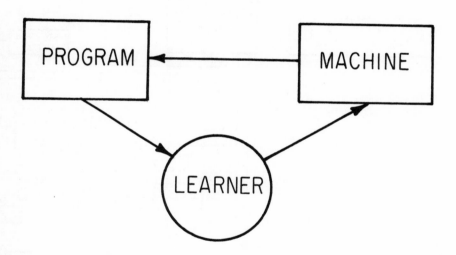

Figure 5-3.   Flow Chart Illustrating Learner-Machine-Program
Relationships. (From Stolurow, "Teaching by Machine," p. 5.)

It was Heinich who in 1962, saw instructional technology as a shift in emphasis being applied not only to the solution of classroom instructional problems but at the curriculum determination and planning levels as well.[30] However, the level of thinking among educators at this time was better exemplified by a Department of Audiovisual Instruction task force in 1963. In speaking of a systems design to instruction in public education they said: "No such model exists as yet . . . some scattered efforts have

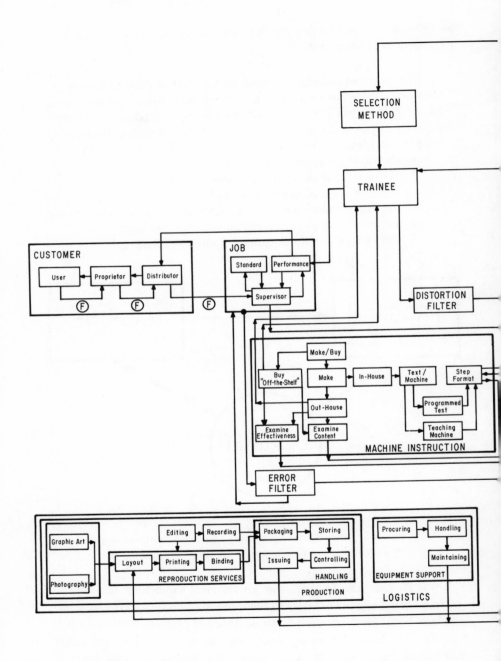

Figure 5-4. Flow Chart Illustrating the Training System Model in
Business and Industry (1963).

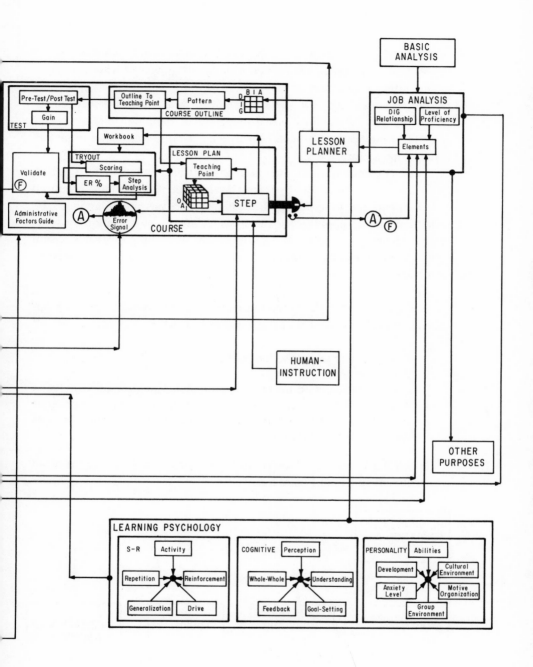

BASIC ANALYSIS

JOB ANALYSIS
DIG Relationship
Level of Proficiency
Elements

COURSE OUTLINE
Pre-Test/Post Test
Gain
TEST
Outline To Teaching Point
Pattern
B I A
D
I
G

Workbook

TRYOUT
Scoring
ER %
Step Analysis

Validate
F

LESSON PLAN
Teaching Point
O
A
STEP

LESSON PLANNER

Administrative Factors Guide
A
Error Signal
COURSE

A F

HUMAN-INSTRUCTION

OTHER PURPOSES

LEARNING PSYCHOLOGY

S-R
Activity
Repetition
Reinforcement
Generalization
Drive

COGNITIVE
Perception
Whole-Whole
Understanding
Feedback
Goal-Setting

PERSONALITY
Abilities
Development
Cultural Environment
Anxiety Level
Motive Organization
Group Environment

attempted to coordinate programmed instruction with other media."[31] (Note that programmed instruction is improperly equated with media as a thing, rather than a process.)

For systems design 1963 was a significant year. Silvern developed the following general training system model "as a stepping stone to specific SYSTEM models for particular areas and for rapid translation to mathematical model form."

The Systems Analysis Committee of the Educational Media Council, with the assistance of the Systems Development Corporation, produced "A Proposal for Long-Range Educational Analysis and Planning." Its objective was "to apply systems analysis techniques to education for long-range planning purposes and as a means whereby top-level decision makers may assess the value of alternative solutions to initial problems in American education."[32]

Gabriel Ofiesh has described the elements of the systems approach applied to the development of instructional materials as:

1. The definition in precise terms of each person's job.
2. A task analysis.
3. A specification of performance requirements and tolerance limits.
4. A statement of the necessary interactions and communications to be carried out between groups, each requirement established to meet the predetermined system goal. . . .[33]

Ofiesh illustrates the relationships between the various functions of an instructional system in Figure 5-5.[34]

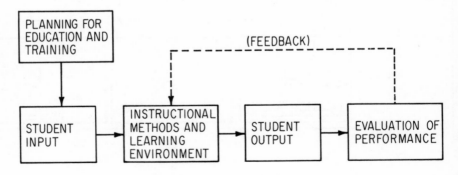

Figure 5-5. Flow Chart Illustrating Functional Relationships—U.S. Air Force (1964).

Stolurow, in a paper at a conference in 1963 on *New Dimensions for Research in Educational Media Implied by the "Systems" Approach to Instruction,* identified a phenomenon that frightened a number of teachers when he said: "Many of the current efforts to develop models of instruction were encouraged, if not forced, by the use of one of the so-called media rather than a live teacher to perform the instructional functions." Significant suggestions derived from this conference were utilization of the systems approach in curriculum development and the application of operational analysis to total school system development.[35]

In 1964 an Air Force workshop produced "A Model for Designing Instructional Systems," shown in Figure 5-6:

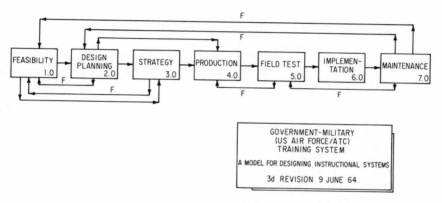

Figure 5-6.   Flow Chart Illustrating a Model for Designing Instructional Systems in the U.S. Air Force at the First Level of Detail. (Silvern et al., 1964.)

During the middle 1960s Robert Smith assessed the state of the art in instructional systems design. His report was produced under a contract with the Department of the Army in 1964-65 under the title, "The Design of Instructional Systems." His *Annotated Bibliography on the Design of Instructional Systems* detailed the available literature. Some of his other publications include: *Controlling the Quality of Training,* Technical Report 65-6, June 1965; *An Annotated Bibliography on Proficiency Measurement for Training Quality Control,* Research Memorandum, June 1964: *The Development of Training Objectives,* Research Bulletin II, June 1964; and *An Annotated Bibliography on the Determination of Training Objectives,* Research Memorandum, June 1964.

Smith identifies the essential functions of an instruction system as:

1. The development of training objectives based on the job for which the student is being trained.
2. The practice of task performance until the student has attained the objective.
3. The practice of knowledges and skills which are components of the task.
4. The presentation of knowledge to the student.
5. Controlling student activity so that it may be directed maximally to the task of learning.
6. Controlling quality of training by means of a quality control system.[36]

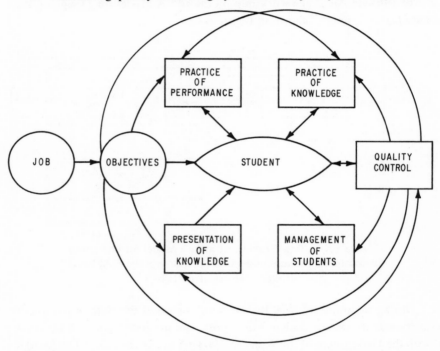

Figure 5-7.   A Model of an Instructional System. (From Smith,
Design of Instructional Systems, p. 4a.)

Since the mid 1960s much has been said about system, systems analysis, systems approach, input, output, feedback, modeling, and other "buzz words." In 1968 Silvern, in *Educational Technology*, attempted to clarify the "systems approach." Again in June of 1969, a special issue of *Educational Technology* devoted to systems techniques was published. Dr. Silvern served as special issue editor. He said:

It is obvious that the *systems approach* has been written about, referred to, and even crudely defined by many individuals specializing in this field. Now, all of this frantic dissemination has culminated in a confused combination of notions, ideas, views, positions, and concepts without principles or practices.[37]

In this publication Silvern attempts to clarify the confusion through the presentation of nine papers each applying systems theory to real-life situations. I reviewed each model presented in this issue and selected certain general systems principles applicable to the model developed in this chapter.

Principle 1: The greater the degree of wholeness in the system, the more efficient the system. A system may be said to possess a high degree of wholeness if when any part of a subsystem is altered all other parts of all other subsystems are affected.

Principle 2: The greater the degree of systemization, the more efficient the operation of the system. Systemization refers to the degree of strength in the signal paths or relationships among parts of the system.

Principle 3: The greater the degree of compatibility between system and environment, the more effective the system. A system should be constructed in such a way as to *match* a given environment.

Principle 4: The greater the degree of optimization, the more effective the system. Optimization is defined as the degree of congruence between system synthesis and system purpose.[38]

IDENTIFICATION OF SYSTEMS MODELS APPLIED TO INSTRUCTION

In selecting examples of a systems approach applied to instruction, the criteria specified in the definition of "systems approach" in this work were utilized:

1. Statement of objectives
2. Delineation of constraints
3. Establishment of measures of effectiveness
4. Synthesis of alternate solutions
5. Establishment of cost elements
6. Cost-effectiveness analysis to establish trade-offs
7. Continuing evaluation and feedback.

The operational examples selected for inclusion represent the state of the art in instructional systems applications. Other more sophisticated theoretical models exist, but as yet are untried in an operational setting and therefore have not been included.

Purdue Audio-Tutorial System, Purdue University, Purdue, Indiana

Dr. Samuel Postlethwait, a professor in the Biological Sciences Department at Purdue University, in an attempt to help some of the less able students in his freshman botany class, taped supplementary lectures for them. Any student could come in at anytime between 7:30 a.m. and 11:30 a.m. and from 12 N. to 11:30 p.m. on Sundays to listen to these lectures on audio tape. Although the first tapes were just lectures, soon pictures and diagrams were added and the tapes became more tutorial in nature. By the end of the first semester of the 1961-62 academic year, Dr. Postlethwait, on an individual basis through the tapes, had each student identifying the parts of plants which the student held in his hand, performing correlated experiments from the laboratory manual, and working with other materials to help him learn. The taped discussion, the materials, laboratory experiments and textbook were integrated as learning packages on a weekly basis. A student could now pass the weekly quiz without attending a single formal session of the course. This "audio-tutorial" instruction was so well received and the students performed so well that during the second semester 36 students pursued all of their instruction in this "programmed" format on audio tape. This group met with the instructor only once each week to take the weekly quiz and for a discussion. These students did just as well on the exams as others in the course. The freshman course in botany for the 1962-63 academic year was restructured along audio-tutorial lines entirely.[39] The course has evolved into three major study sessions:

1. A general assembly session (GAS) scheduled one hour per week and involving all students.
2. An integrated quiz session (IQS) scheduled one-half hour per week and involving eight students.
3. An independent study session (ISS) unscheduled but the equivalent of four hours of conventional instruction and involving all students in audio-tutorial study.[40]

Another type of activity, a small assembly session, is normally held each week also. The schedule depends on the course and the amount of time required in discussion activity.

The *general assembly session* provides an opportunity for motivation, orientation, guest lectures, viewing long films, announcements, and other activities which can best be accomplished in a large group assembly. It is conducted by the senior instructor in the course and makes use of common audio visual devices such as 2 x 2 slides, 16mm movie film, overhead projector, blackboard and television when available.

The *integrated quiz session* involves eight students and one instructor seated informally around a table. The instructor is provided with those items included in the learning center the preceding week and uses them as a device for quizzing and discussion of the week's subject matter. Each student receives, in his turn, one of the items and is expected to identify the item, its role in the week's work, and discuss how it fulfills this role. The items are delivered in a programmed fashion to a student selected at random and all students may contribute to the discussion when appropriate. A student is subjectively placed in one of three grade categories based on his performance. If the instructor is favorably impressed, he is placed in a category of excellent and is assigned a score of 9. If the instructor is not much impressed, the student is placed in the category of mediocre and is given a score of 7. If the instructor is depressed, the student is placed in the category of poor and is assigned a score of 5 or less. Grades may be raised or lowered by the student's further contribution during the discussion.

The *independent study session* is at the convenience of the student in a Learning Center. The Learning Center is provided with individual booths equipped with tape players and other materials appropriate to the week's work. Equipment and other materials too bulky for inclusion in the booths are placed on an experiment table. The student checks in on arrival and checks out on departure on a specially prepared card. The card is used for booth assignment and as a record of the student's participation. There are 30 booths to serve up to 600 students. Within the booth the student is tutored by the senior instructor through a complete series of learning experiences. These may include a lecture introducing the subject for the week, reading paragraphs from the text or *Scientific American* articles, doing laboratory exercises and experiments from their study guide, viewing of 8mm films, discussions with fellow students and instructors, study of microscopic specimens, and any other kind of learning experiences appropriate to the nature of the week's objectives. Any or all learning events may be repeated or omitted commensurate with the student's needs. Each student proceeds at his own pace and studies until he has mastered the subject matter for the week. An instructor is available to give assistance at all times. The Learning Center is open from 7:30 a.m. until 10:30 p.m. Monday through Friday.[41]

The *small assembly session* is to bring together a small number of students with an experienced discussion leader to do many of the items ordinarily accomplished in a conventional recitation session. It is a scheduled session which meets routinely each week and is in charge of the same instructor throughout the semester.[42]

The instructor in the small assembly session becomes well acquainted with students, keeps up with student progress, provides counseling, and leads discussions and conducts activities. The characteristics of the small assembly session are: no rigid format, adjusts to situation and nature of learning, and typically wide variety of activities.[43]

When a student registers at Purdue for freshman botany he is scheduled each week for one hour of GAS and two hours of SAS, only one of which is used. The remaining four hours are to be used for independent study in the learning center. To serve the 150 to 480 students enrolled in this course, a professor as senior instructor, a full-time instructor, four teaching assistant equivalents (actually working ¼, ¾, or full time), two graduate assistants, and the equivalent of a half-time secretary are employed.[44]

Oakland Community College, Bloomfield Hills, Michigan

In describing the instructional system employed at Oakland Community College, Tirrell, its innovative former president, speaks of using "a learner-centered instructional systems approach":

Before we designed our instructional program, we made a review of literature—supplemented in some cases by interviews and observational visits—in three areas:

1. Principles of learning.
2. Class size and space and time utilization.
3. Innovations in teaching—including, for example, some of the work at Florida Atlantic University, System Development Corporation's computer-based classroom, and, of course, Professor Postlethwait's work at Purdue.

As a result of this investigation and review, we concluded that there are three major factors in learning what must be recognized in any plan that we might develop:

1. Motivation is primary.
2. The active learner learns most—and in a shorter time.
3. Feedback is necessary to accelerate and raise the quality of learning.

On the basis of these findings, we developed a plan which is a learner-centered, systems approach to instruction and which features a learning laboratory and feedback.[45]

In outlining the significant steps in Oakland's approach, Tirrell lists:

1. Terminal objectives for *all* courses are identified, and defined in behavioral terms. Terminal Objectives or Terminal Performance Specifications (TPS)—what the student should understand, comprehend, or demonstrate knowledge of at the end of his course of instruction—are prepared by each faculty member having responsibility for a course offering. [Figure 5-8] Generally, each unit (covering a 1-2 week period) of the course is designed to accomplish a specific TPS. Each unit has a criterion test which is used to evaluate achievement of the TPS by the student.
2. Once the TPSs are documented, attention is given to the identification of the Interim Objectives or the Interim Performance Specifications (IPS) and detailed learning steps. [Figure 5-9] These are sequenced meaningfully, and wherever possible time-based. The IPSs are ordered from the simple to complex or from the unfamiliar to the new as in the microprogrammed book, with an attempt made to assign study times appropriate for achieving them. Since the objectives are made explicit, the most appropriate media can be selected. These range from mimeographed essays with study questions to audiotapes, integrated text readings, textbooks, journals, magazine and newspaper articles, visual displays, 8mm single-concept films, film strips and 35mm slides, laboratory experimental set-ups, and of course, programmed texts. Materials are constructed or selected so to allow for active response by the learner, and immediate feedback to him.
3. An attempt is made to keep the learner aware of what the sequence of instruction will be, in most cases, by furnishing him with a study guide or checklist for each unit of a course. This guide lists the general and intermediate objectives that he will be expected to achieve,

[Figure 5-10] and the learning steps he must follow. [Figure 5-11]
Thus, he is kept informed at each step within a unit of a course what
he will be tested on and when, so that he can schedule his time in
the learning laboratory—as it is known at Oakland Community College—on a self-paced basis.

4. The overall approach—of stating objectives in behavioral terms, of
   organizing and sequencing media and study time, of the learner
   keeping himself informed, and of promoting his active participation
   in the learning experience—is then evaluated regularly and frequently by calling for the criterion responses appropriate. These are
   embodied in oral, performance and written tests.

The implementation of all these instructional programmed features at Oakland Community College constitutes a unique learner-
centered instructional systems approach. Such implementation has
resulted in many innovations in the appearance of our facilities, and
the conduct of our educational practices. Learners at Oakland Community College follow a self-paced and self-scheduled plan of study
in accomplishing most of their program/course requirements.

This has created the need for unique facilities unlike the conventional classrooms. The result has been the Oakland Community College "learning laboratory" which houses study carrels rather than
traditional student chair-desks. When needed, laboratories of the
more traditional type provide an opportunity for the student to apply
what he has learned to practical problems, and find unique solutions.
While in the learning laboratory itself, tutors are available to answer
questions and offer other help on a one-to-one basis. If the learners'
need is more extensive, individual conference areas adjoin the laboratories.

If at the end of a unit of instruction the student requires individual
clarification of an even more extensive nature, or has formulated an
individual project which he would like to carry out, or has begun to
think about career opportunities, faculty with extensive experience
in the student's field of interest can be consulted. An effort is made
to see that faculty advisors and laboratory tutors keep scheduled
hours to assist the student. Facilities for enriching subject matter,
motivating further inquiry, clarifying special issues, allowing group
discussion and evaluating the student's progress are also provided.
These needs are met in either small assembly sessions or large general assembly sessions. In the SAS, 5 to 6 students meet with the
tutor for seminar-type discussions and, for example, case-study
solving. At the large GAS they meet in groups of 30 or more with
an instructor to hear guest speakers, view group movies, or take unit
quizzes or course tests.

Course No. 84.251
Course Title General Psychology   Functional Performance Analysis — A
Unit No. 2   Unit Title Heredity, Maturation & Adolescence
     Unit Description:

Coordinator A. Ugelow
Date 1/66

Assessment by the student of the interaction of heredity, maturation, and environmental influences in individual differences. Assignment of relative weights to the effects of early vs. late experience especially in adolescence.

	Hours Alloted
	14

Terminal Performance Specification

The student will identify, at the objective test level, the major hereditary, maturational, and environmental determinants of individuality in general and of adolescence in particular. No reference materials will be provided at the time of testing.

Examples of Criterion Questions

1. For each of the instances of behavior or bodily characteristics below, indicate by the appropriate letter, the factor which best accounts for it:

   (H): the individual's unique and original hereditary make-up

   (M): the orderly maturational sequence common to all normal humans and different from that of other organisms

   (E): the presence of a specific environmental influence or demand which may have altered the natural course of events

    1.1   The gradual onset of understandable English in infants as opposed to Spanish

    1.2   The absence of skin pigment in a child of parents having normal skin pigment

    1.3   The absence of an "instinct of self-preservation" in soldiers who risk their lives

2. Problems of adjustment relating to sexual development, emancipation from home, relations with age-mates, and perception of self are created by_____changes occurring in adolescence.

Figure 5-8.   Terminal Performance Specifications, Oakland Community College. Copyright OCC—1966.

75

Course No. 84.251
Course Title __General__ Psychology #2
Terminal Performance Specifications #2: Heredity, Maturation, and Adolescence

Functional Performance Analysis – B

Coordinator __A. Ugelow__
Date __1/66__

Interim Performance Specifications		Learning Steps		Criterion Performance Evaluation (Responses)	Media Selection	Time Required
No.		No.				
2.1	The student will recognize that there is an interaction of heredity, maturation, and environment.	1.	Identify and define at preview level that heredity, maturation, and learning have to do with individuality.	1. Which of the factors – heredity, maturation, environment – best accounts for the pre-valence of musical talent in the Bach family in all probability.	Tape Hand-out Text reading	2 Hrs.
		2.	Explain the nature – nurture interaction.	2. What effect might the kind of early schooling received by the various Bachs at home have had on their interest in music? Is it still legitimate to ascribe such talent strictly to heredity?	" "	
		3.	Extract one effect of heredity, one of maturation, and one of learning in an instance of achievement by members of an outstanding family.		Small Assembly	
2.2	The student will solve simple problems using the dominance and recession tables of heredity.	1.	Define phenotype and genotype.	True or False? 1. The phenotype is the basis for genetic qualities that may or may not be displayed while the genotype is the actual trait which is displayed. True or False?	Text Reading Hand-out	4 Hrs.
		2.	Distinguish between domin-ance and recessiveness.	2. A person's phenotype reflects one or more dominant genes.		
		3	Explain sex determination hereditarily by reference to X and Y chromosomes.	3. Diagram the dominance-recession table to show the four possible genotypes which insure that the probability of a boy or girl being born is always 50/50.		
		4.	Distinguish between different organismic characteristics on heredity vs. environment basis.	4. If a boy looks like his father we may say that he has ____ the resemblance, but if he has his father's temper most likely this characteristic was ____.		
	–continued–		–continued–	– continued –	–continued–	–continued –

REW:k:s
12/17/65

Figure 5-9. Interim Performance Specifications, Oakland Community College. Copyright OCC—1966.

TITLE: Unit 2, Heredity, Maturation, and Adolescence CODE: 84.251.2

GENERAL OBJECTIVE:

The student shall assess the interaction of heredity, maturation, and their interaction with environment in making the individual unique. He shall interpret the special problems of adolescence. He will do so at the objective test level and without the use of reference.

INTERMEDIATE OBJECTIVES:

2.1 The student shall recognize that there is an important interaction of heredity, maturation, and environment through learning which means we cannot assign individual differences to either heredity or maturation alone.

2.2 The student shall distinguish phenotype and genotype, dominance and recession, and solve simple problems using the dominance and recession table.

2.3 The student shall define maturation and shall trace the maturation of motor responses, sensitivity, and early emotion.

2.4 The student shall identify major areas of environmental influence on the developing child: toilet training and feeding, relations with parents, age-mates and siblings, and schooling.

2.5 The student shall identify the major bodily changes in adolescence and interpret their significance for problems of teen-age having to do with sexual development, independence, and emancipation from home, age-mates, and juvenile delinquency.

The first step is to read the above objectives. Then turn the page and perform each step in the sequence indicated.

Figure 5-10. General and Intermediate Objectives, Oakland Community College. Copyright OCC—1966.

	PROGRAM	MEDIA	TIME
		Hand-out Plus	
2.1	**Major Determinants of Individuality**		2 hrs.
	1. Obtain Tape 84.252.2 . Listen to this tape and take notes, if necessary. Return tape when done.	Tape	
	2. Read Section 2.1 and 2.1.1 in your hand-out. Keep Hilgard handy. Refer to p. 433, Fig. 15—5, as directed.	Text	
	3. Do the exercise in Section 2.1.1 of your hand-out. Ask your Instructor to schedule a Small Assembly on this	Small Assembly	
2.2	**Significance of Heredity for Individuality**		4 hrs.
	1. In Hilgard, read Chapter 15, pp. 423 – 425 (middle)	Text	
	2. Read Section 2.2 through 2.2.1 in your hand-out.		
	3. Do the exercise in Section 2.2.2 of your hand-out and read the Conclusion in Section 2.2.3.		
	4. Make note of questions to be taken up at your General Assembly Session.	General Assembly	
2.3	**The Concept of Maturation**		3 hrs.
	1. In Hildgard, read Chapter 3, pp. 69 – 74.	Text	
	2. Read Section 2.3 in your hand-out through 2.3.5.		
	3. Do the exercise in Section 2.3.6 of your hand-out and read the Conclusion in Section 2.3.7.		
2.4	**Major Environmental Influences In Early Development**		1 hr.
	1. Read Section 2.4 through 2.4.3 in your hand-out.		
2.5	**Bodily Changes in Adolescence**		4 hrs.
	1. Obtain Tape 84.252.2 once more. Locate the section on it entitled "Introduction to Adolescence" (If you need help in finding it, see your instructor.) Listen to this tape and take notes if necessary. Return tape when done.	Tape	
	2. Read Section 2.5 in your hand-out.		
	3. In Hilgard, read Chapter 4, pp. 102 – 110 (middle).		
	4. Do the excercise in your hand-out, Section 2.5.1.		
	At the conclusion of this unit you will have your first block test covering Units 1 and 2. Your Instructor will announce the date.		

Figure 5-11.   Learning Steps, Oakland Community College.
Copyright OCC—1966.

The unique specification of the learning experience at Oakland Community College and the availability of extensive course-planning and implementation documents will eventually enable public evaluation of our program and has already provided an invaluable opportunity to work cooperatively with commercial firms in the preparation of a portion of our program texts/booklets. The highly detailed performance specifications developed by Oakland Community College are presented to the college's contractors, Litton Industries (which utilizes the linear instruction programming format) and Howard & Smith (which utilizes a tight branching format) to undertake the programming of some 132 unit-length, instructional programmed texts/booklets for some 20 college course areas, based on our unique requirements.

In summary, the application of the learner-centered instructional systems approach at Oakland Community College was adapted to reach more students with less instructional personnel, promote the learning of more information with greater comprehension, and in less time.[46]

Figure 5-8 is a sample terminal performance specification, Figure 5-9 is an interim performance specification, Figure 5-10 shows a sample of a general and intermediate objectives, and Figure 5-11 shows the learning steps.

Continuation Education System Development Project, La Puente, Calif.

The overall objective of the CEDS project, which began in 1967, is "to provide the Valley High School (a continuation school) with a "self-sustaining capability to manage the day-to-day conduct, and to continue the development of instructional programs that will meet the individual requirements for each continuation student. The purpose of continuation education is to provide such students with an acceptable alternative to the traditional high school. The program must be counseling-oriented rather than subject matter-oriented, providing an individualized approach to the learn-needs of each youngster." This three-year project was to:

Year 1. specify the requirements for instructional programs at Valley High;

Year 2: design a system to manage the programs;

Year 3: install the system.

Year 1 (1967-68):

During the first year the needs of continuation students were identified. The tasks involved were:

1. To determine the skills and knowledges required for entry and minimum success in the next place that the student is likely to go when he leaves the program.
2. To determine the present capabilities of the continuation student. How far is he from mastery of the knowledge and skills specified? This was done through performance testing.
3. The requirements and capabilities were then compared and a description of instructional needs derived.
4. An assessment was then made of the human and material resources available to meet these needs. What were the constraints in evidence?
5. The final task was a definition of priorities and the selection of a sequence of instructional objectives. The cost of meeting each instructional need was compared with some measure of benefit to be derived. Based upon this analysis, priorities were set.

Year 2 (1968-69):

During the second year a system was designed to meet the performance requirements identified during Year 1, specifying all needed activities, personnel skills, and facilities. The following tasks were performed:

1. Tests of student performance were collected from publishers, Job Corps Centers, other continuation and regular high schools, and where necessary, drafted by the project staff.
2. Instructional activities were specified to facilitate student learning—specified terminal performance. The resources required for each activity were identified from off-the-shelf material. Local production was limited where possible to tailoring and assembling ready-made component parts.
3. Management activities in the area of instructional planning were specified. A study was made of the kind of information and decision-making actions which will be required if each student is to identify his needs and choose an appropriate instructional program.
4. The final task was the identification of logistical support tasks and resources. Required personnel skills, materials, supplies, equipment, and space were compared with those resources already on hand to determine deficiencies.

Year 3 (1969-70):

During this year subsystems designed during Year 2 will be implemented and evaluated. This involves acquiring needed personnel skills and media, trying out and testing performance, comparing the results with pre-established criteria, and recommending changes as necessary.

Year 4 (1970-71):

A tryout of the total system will be conducted by the permanent school staff. Subsystems found faulty during the testing period of Year 3 will be upgraded and the successful interaction of all segments of the program will become the major area of concern. As in previous tryouts, the end behavior of the student will stand as the final criterion of the effectiveness of the program. The same cycle of testing and revision will be repeated in each subsequent year, and the system will continue to sense and respond to the need for change.[47]

The Job Corps—Office of Economic Opportunity, Washington, D.C.

The Job Corps was created by the Economic Opportunity Act of 1964. Its broad objectives, general target population, and basic environmental structure were established by law in the following words:

> . . . to prepare for the responsibilities of citizenship and to increase the employability of young men and young women, aged sixteen through twenty-one, by providing them in rural and urban residential centers with education, vocational training, useful work experience, including work directed toward the conservation of natural resources and other appropriate activities. [Economic Opportunity Act of 1964, P.L. 88-452, 42 USC2700 *et. seq.,* Title I, Part A, Section 101.]

Two major program distinctions were made. First, separate programs were established for men and for women. Second, programs for men were divided into those conducted by conservation centers and those conducted by urban centers. Conservation centers were to focus on provision of worthwhile work experience for corps members through helping the De-partments of Agriculture and Interior in conservation work. Urban centers were to be sophisticated vocational skills training centers. These distinctions had a major effect on the structure of curricula.

The following steps were followed in the development of the men's programs: (1) analysis of target population, (2) delineation of constraints—environmental, and (3) specification of objectives stated in terms of the behavior expected of Job Corps graduates.[48]

Conservation Centers. In implementing these objectives, detailed behavior analyses were conducted that specified instructional objectives as steps toward reaching larger end objectives. The characteristics of the youth entering a conservation center served as the starting point from which he was to proceed up the steps of behavioral instructional objectives to the top or graduate objectives in each program area.[49]

Urban Centers. Initially the objectives for urban centers were specified in only general terms. Unlike the conservation center effort where Job Corps professionals specified end objectives and worked hand in hand with contractors in specifying instructional objectives for each program and curriculum component, the mandate to specify objectives for their efforts was given to the individual contractors responsible for the several Urban Centers. The contractors were expected to produce corpsman graduates who could get and hold a job in the vocational area for which they were trained and who had improved their academic levels, if possible, to high school equivalency. Decisions concerning what behaviors had to be developed to reach these general goals were left to the contractors.[50]

After three years of independent development and operation, Job Corps made the decision to specify standard objectives for all urban centers.[51]

Development of a program structure was undertaken with the instructional objective as the basic unit:

Name of Level *Definition*

Instructional   An instructional objective is a statement
Objective   describing a behavior, the conditions
                 under which it is learned, and the
                 method for determining that learner has
                 acquired the behavior.

Milestone	A milestone is a group of instructional objectives that have similar operations or related content.
Module	A module is a unit of instruction consisting of related milestones that prepares a corpsman for a specific type or level of job or other complex of behavior.
Program	A program is a course of instruction that covers several modules or jobs in the same occupational grouping or related complexes of behavior.
Cluster	A cluster contains two or more related programs.[52]

An example of the implementation of the urban center structure in the vocational area may be helpful. The following is drawn from the Food Service Cluster:

Instructional Objective	Given a recipe, skillet, fork, spatula, shortening and range, the corpsman will prepare and cook a plain omelet. He will combine eggs and milk in a bowl and whip. He will then place the mixture in a properly heated and greased skillet. The omelet will be folded when coagulation occurs and cooked until ready to serve. The finished omelet will be light and fluffy, yellow in color, neatly folded and well heated. The corpsman will prepare at least 10 omelets successfully in the judgment of his instructor.
Milestone	Breakfast Foods
Module	Short Order Cook
Program	Cooking
Cluster	Food Service

The example gives one of several objectives for the milestone, which is one of several milestones in the module, which is one of several modules in the program. The cluster is composed of cooking, baking, waiting, and meat-cutting programs.[53]

Instructional content: This content consists of the information and experiences necessary to develop the behavior of the learner from entering level to output or objective level.[54]

Urban centers, unlike conservation centers, were responsible for their own instructional content determinations. Creation of selection of experiences, information, texts, manuals, and supportive materials was left wholly to the discretion and skill of the centers, although they were provided with general guidelines and monitoring at headquarters. A general consideration in the selection of instructional content for Job Corps has been maximizing the probability of achieving specifically stated behavioral objectives in minimum time. Efficiency has been an important factor, because retention of corpsmen in programs is difficult and expensive. Corpsmen, as a target group, require immediate "pay-off," or relevance.[55]

Methods and media: Alternative methods and media were evaluated in terms of relative potential for appropriate message presentation and provision of feedback to the learners. They were considered in terms of the "target populations" characteristics, the nature of the instructional objectives, and, of course, the environmental constraints on instruction. Cost efficiency was also an important consideration for Job Corps as a Federal Program.[56]

> Instruction was "programmed" in the broadest sense of the term. The Corpsman Advisory System (CAS) was a major methodological innovation initiated in the Conservation Centers. This system was designed to make each corpsman the focus of his own training and educational experience. The system made it possible for his progress in all program areas to be monitored on a regular basis and for him to be kept informed of his progress and advised concerning his immediate and longer-term future.[57]

Job Corps has attempted to systematically consider and develop (1) the nature of the target population, (2) the constraints in the learning environment, (3) the objectives of instruction, (4) the necessary instructional content, and (5) the methods,[58] as well as the way all of these interact in the development of an instruction system including programs and curricula.

Colorado Mountain College

The instructional systems model used on the two campuses of Colorado Mountain College represents a second generation of the Oakland Community College system with modifications.

Like Oakland, every course at Colorado Mountain College, from liberal arts through career programs, was designed to produce predictable learner behavior through the utilization of a variety of learning strategies (methods and media).

The late Dr. Joseph U. Davenport, the first president of Colorado Mountain College, said:

> The successful implementation of the independent study model of instruction requires careful integration of all of its operating components into one carefully designed system. Since the ultimate objective is to produce successful achievement by individual learners, it is necessary to identify those skills and knowledges necessary to the success of an individual on the job, or for advancement into institutions of higher education. All instructional programs will be designed as self-contained instructional systems. The learner is provided with a complete list of all course objectives, intermediate objectives, learning steps, and the methods and media to be used in each learning step. Consequently, he knows at all times where he is in the program, where the program is leading him, what is expected of him, how he will determine when he has achieved the stated objectives, and the criteria by which his level of performance will be evaluated. The great efficacy of this methodology rests upon the following tested tenets of learning behavior:

The Ten Tenets of the Learner-Oriented Instruction

1. Small Learning Steps (each step covers a single item of instruction).
2. Active Participation (learner makes specific response or action for each step).
3. Immediate Confirmation (learner given correct answer to each question immediately after his response).
4. Self-paced (learning activity, path, and pace under learner's control).
5. Variety of Method/Media (utilize full range of learning methods and learning tools).
6. Instructor-learner Dialogs (frequent small group sessions and constant availability of tutoring).
7. Programs Tailored to Individual Learner (no two learners reach terminal objectives by same path).

8. Meaningful Terminal Objectives (Program objectives based on "Need-to-Know" or "Need-to-Do" criteria only).
9. Compatible Physical Environment (environment must produce "approach" behavior in learner).
10. Validation and Evaluation (programs must be continually validated and improved, and learner progress constantly evaluated).

In summary, this approach to learning tells the student what is expected of him, shows him where to obtain the required information and learning tools, provides an atmosphere of encouragement and assistance, and then expects him to demonstrate performance consistent, always, with his instruction.[59]

The Southern California Regional Occupational Center's Multimedia Remote Access Educational System (SCROC), Torrence, California

In 1969 six school districts, serving an area with more than a half-million people in the Los Angeles area, entered into a joint venture. The purpose of the venture was to train students for entry into the job market and for retaining of adults for new jobs or upgrading in present jobs.

The objectives of SCROC are:

1. To expand the occupational and vocational opportunities available to residents of the *joint powers* area, thereby increasing the employability of both our youth and adult populations.
2. To aggressively pursue a partnership between education and industry.
3. To create a truly innovative and flexible institution, capable of quick action in meeting the challenging needs of a dynamic economy.
4. To develop a flexible, efficient, practical approach to individualized training.
5. To assume responsibility for those who can profit from training by providing:

   Both training and retraining for persons who have already entered the labor market but are unemployed or underemployed.

   Rehabilitation training for the physically handicapped.

   Realistic and up-to-date programs for in-school and out-of-school youth who wish to acquire a saleable skill.

Special training programs for persons who have academic or socio-economic handicaps that prevent them from succeeding in regular training programs.[60]

In order to implement a program to meet these objectives, the SCROC laid out five steps or areas of activity:

1. Employ the systems approach to define the occupational educational systems objectives, task analysis, behavioral specification, and related terminal behavior statements.[61] This was accomplished through:

   —task analysis of the occupational skills to be offered at the Center;

   —the analysis and identification of the specific skills;

   —a specification of the terminal behavior;

   —the derivation of the sub-behaviors making up the terminal behavior and specify as objectives;

   —an identification of the key teaching points upon which the development of the instructional program is based.

2. Define and analyze the educational systems' operating strategy, select the subject matter design formats and the appropriate media for transmission. This was accomplished through an analysis of the product of identifying the key teaching points mentioned above. Software was designed and formats thus derived were studied.

3. Produce, package, and test self-instructional media modules as software items that will be used to test out and fill the hardware system.

4. Select, design, and implement a full remote access retrieval system with associated hardware, software, and related items. The system specified had to service the following functions:

   —production of original media input programmed materials, as well as the correlation of stored materials;

   —storage of media materials (in all formats) on source origination equipment.

   —distribution of the stored materials to remote station locations such as: the individual student study carrel, classroom retrieval systems, skill and shop retrieval systems, and teacher design retrieval systems.

   —retrieval of random dial access and audio-video display of any stored materials from any remote station under two present use conditions.[62]

5. Implement, operate, and manage a system of self-instruction in order for students to learn at their own pace and perform under supervision the critical procedures required in each related occupational field.

Once fully developed, what will the operational system look like and what will the student do in order to meet the objectives as established? Arthur M. Suchesk, the manager of the Instructional Media and Systems Division of the Center, describes it this way:

The Center is in the process of designing, developing, and implementing a system whereby a student, after being properly counseled, will have his total occupational curriculum programmed on a plastic punch card. The student, as part of his normal high school day, will attend the Center for a three-hour period during which he will be directed to a study carrel which will have a video and audio display unit. By inserting his plastic curriculum card, a computer will be addressed indicating the student's account. The computer will verify the student is in "good standing" with the Center and will proceed to retrieve via various media formats that portion of the program in which the student is involved. Entering the program at his own inventory level and working at a self-pacing mode, he may elect to recall or request advance information as he so desires.

During his time on this system, he will be under a surveillance and detection system which will in effect monitor his responses. In the event he produces the incorrect responses in a certain predetermined quantity, the system will stop, and an alarm will be issued to a master teacher who will then come on the video screen and have a dialogue with the student. The student will be queried as to why he is having trouble and may be directed to repeat a segment of the program, report to the career advisor's office for a face-to-face meeting, or be told to move to another operation and come back later to partake of a customized prescription loop. The master teacher in the interim, referring to an index which details all known subject matter data in the repository, would select bits and portions that will in effect remedy the student's problem. This new composition, the prescription loop, would be issued to the student when he returns. Upon completion of the prescription loop, the student would continue on his regular assigned program course, progressing through a series of modules and progression tests.

Upon leaving the study carrel, the student would be directed to the hands-on training area where he would proceed to carry on with practical training. In each of the hands-on training areas, study carrel stations would be available where the student could call for review information, specific step-by-step procedure information, catalog, data, and standards information. By picking up a wireless headphone set, and directing the transmission antenna towards his area of work, he could then proceed to accomplish the work while listening to step-by-step instructions through the phones.

The student could also use this system to call for performance standards. After producing his own model, he would be able to check his performance against the proposed standards. Throughout this exercise there will be on-site "instructor monitors" who will be available to provide in-depth direction and counseling to those students requiring it.[63]

Individually Prescribed Instruction (IPI), Oakleaf Elementary School, Baldwin-Whitehall School District

The program initiated in 1963 at the Oakleaf School, a suburb of Pittsburgh, Pennsylvania, is called *individually prescribed instruction* (IPI). It was developed jointly by the Baldwin-Whitehall school district with the assistance of Drs. Glaser, Lindvall, and Bolvin of the Learning Research and Development Center of the University of Pittsburgh.

The project, while beginning in a single "intact" classroom, soon required a more flexible organizational pattern. The experience gained was valuable in the evolution of IPI, which has now spread through the project, "Research for Better Schools," to 170 elementary schools across the country in one or more subject areas.

Characteristics of IPI. IPI is based on a carefully sequenced and detailed listing of behaviorally stated instructional objectives. The objectives are sequenced in a learning hierarchy.

The lesson materials are developed so as to cause the student proceeding through them to meet the objective. The materials, for the most part, are not dependent on the teacher for information presentation, but rather permit the learner to proceed independently.

"Placement instruments" are used to determine grossly where a child should be placed in the learning continuum. The pretest is used in order to determine the specific objective that determines the specific place at which a student should begin.

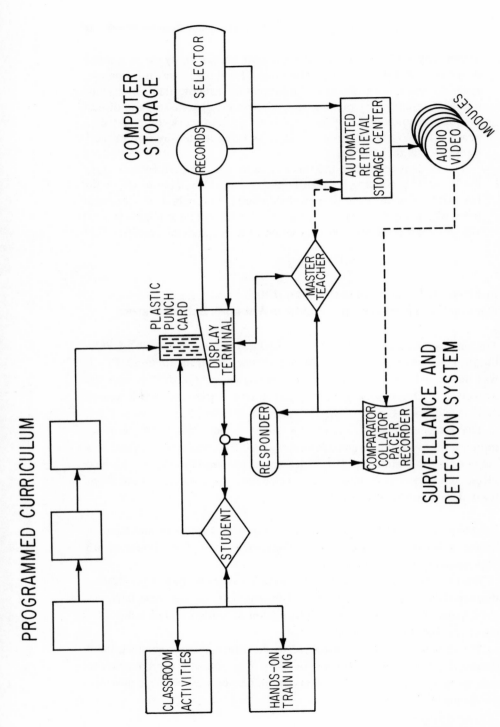

Figure 5-12. Southern California Regional Occupational Center Computer-Managed Multimedia DAIRS Schematic.

A prescription for each student is written, based on his individual needs and interests. At each step along the way the progress of the student is measured toward achievement of the objective through a "curriculum-embedded test" (CET). The CET serves a second function, which is as a pretest to the next objective. If at any point the student ceases to progress toward achieving the objective, the prescription is modified and the student tries again.

At the end of each unit of instruction each student is given an alternate form of the pretest called the post test. This instrument also serves two functions—as a progress or mastery check and as a pretest to the next objective. Records are systematically maintained on the progress of each student, his degree of success with each learning strategy prescribed, and information relative to the specific problem encountered in the learning materials. Information on the specific problem is used in the continuing modification of materials and processes based on this empirical evidence. Information on the progress of each student is used in improving future diagnosis and prescription.

The learning materials were produced and improved in the empirical manner described above through the cooperative efforts of the LRDC staff, the staff of the Oakleaf Elementary School, and later, the commercial publisher.

The activities the teacher performs within IPI are diagrammed in Figure 5-13.

It is my purpose in this section to develop a model of an instructional system which may be used to aid a new institution in employing a systems approach to the development of its instructional program. A model is defined here as "an abstraction of the real world in order to represent reality." This abstraction consists of a graphic and narrative description which may then be used to "exercise," on paper, its components and their interrelationships for modification and adjustment, to insure optimal configuration in meeting established goals.

The model developed in this section was synthesized from an analysis of the operating instructional systems (described in the preceding section), which was selected from theoretical models of instructional systems drawn from the literature, existing technology, the theories of instruction, and the curriculum developed in Chapters 2 and 3. The model is grounded in the philosophy and conclusions of Chapter 4 and provides a basis on which guidelines may be drawn for a new community college.

The development of a "systems approach" to instruction has been traced historically in Chapter 5, with various examples noted. A prominent, gen-

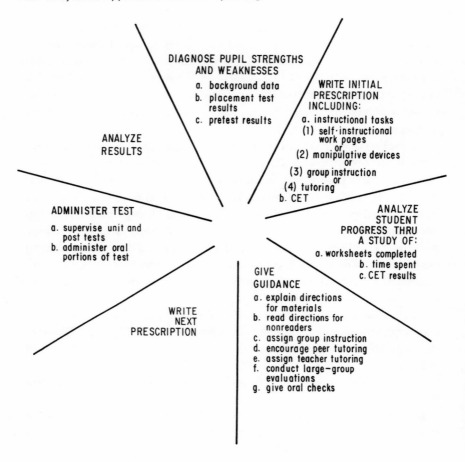

Figure 5-13.   Teacher Functions.

eral model developed by Silvern was singled out for particular attention, since it spawned several operational instruction systems.

Of the seven operational models selected for study, none contained all of the elements suggested in the synthesized model. Each of these operating systems was selected because it represented a fairly complete application of a systems approach. Each was analyzed, as were the various theoretical models reported on, by reduction to their component parts for purposes of study. Additional analyses were derived from a study of the various technologies growing out of the basic sciences and the fields of curriculum and instruction.

The preliminary instructional systems model that is described in the following pages was synthesized from the analyses cited above.

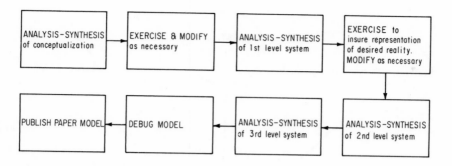

Figure 5-14.   Process of Model Development.

The process I followed was: first, analysis as described; then synthesis of a conceptualization; then analysis of the conceptualization and modification of it; then a synthesis of a first-level system model; and then analysis of this model to insure its representation of the desired reality. A second-level system model was generated and then a third. Finally, the model was "debugged" by processing data through it and modifying it as necessary, in order to take a first step toward validating it.

The type of model I have employed is a flowchart—a graphic analog representing an "ideal" instructional system annotated with verbal description. The blocks in the analog represent significant components of the system and the arrows represent a flow of information/data and products. Feedback loops represent a flow of data used for system adjustment.

The instructional system whose major elements have been diagrammed as *Student, Curriculum, Guidance,* and *Instruction* forms a system whose purpose is to produce a measurable amount of student behavior change (learning) in predetermined directions. It has both subsystems (each function comprises one) and a supra-system, the community college system of which it is but one subsystem.

In Figure 5-15 the community college is graphically displayed as a system receiving inputs from a number of sources outside the system, which are used to modify, create, and otherwise make the system responsive to the needs of the students and the community.

Each arrow represents a flow of information either from or to one of the systems or subsystems.

To illustrate this empirical approach to curriculum development, let us assume that no programs exist in a newly organized community college. The decision as to what to offer would be determined in the occupational

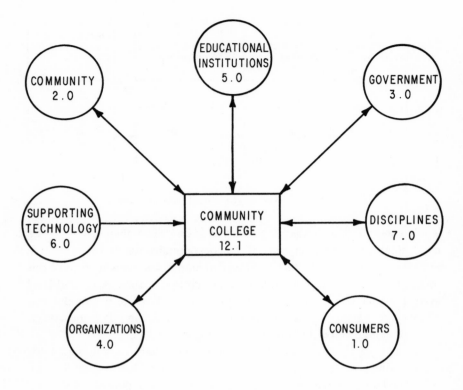

Figure 5-15.   The Model: Community College—Inputs
from Other Systems.

area by ascertaining community and student need and current services by
other agencies, and, where a need exists, establishing programs to meet
the need identified. The procedure?

Stimulate: 1.0 Consumer, 2.0 Community, and 3.0 Educational Institutions to provide inputs to 12.1 the community college.

The same basic approach should be utilized to determine the *content* of
the programs thus derived: Stimulate 2.0 Community (advisory committees), 4.0 Organizations (unions, guilds, professional societies, etc.), and
5.0 Government (federal, state, and local) to identify standards; and 2.0
Community (perform analyses of human activity).

All programs would be updated on a continuing basis by stimulating 1.0
Consumers (graduate follow-up testings; surveying employers of graduates; and surveying graduate activities through the "community" in which
the graduate resides, professionally, geographically, and through service).

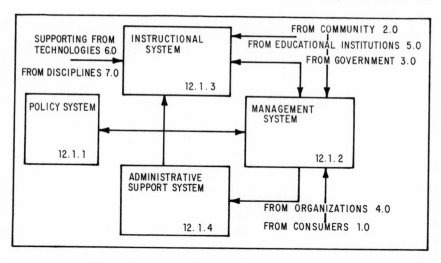

Figure 5-16. The Model: Community College.

In Figure 5-16 the flow of this information from outside the system is shown inputing to each function within the instructional and management systems. Since the focus of this book is the instructional system, the community college—although referred to as a system—is in fact a supra-system, and the guidance function within the instructional system, itself a system, is described as a function or subsystem.

Due to the characteristic interrelationships in all systems, it is necessary to study at least the principal systems (policy, management, instructional, and administrative support) within the supra-system (community college) in order to analyze and model its operation adequately. It is interesting to note that there are no direct flows of information from the policy system to either the instructional or the administrative support systems, nor vice versa.

Figure 5-17 shows the relationship of the functions, the inputs, and the outputs. The circled information refers to the particular subsystem that interfaces or joins with them and from which data comes or goes depending on the direction of the arrowhead.

Inputs entering the management system are analyzed in order to formulate policy recommendations to the governing body of the college regarding any elements or procedures of the instructional system—for example, a new curriculum in data processing; any element in the administrative support system (e.g., the construction of a mobile facility to house an electrical repair program which would travel outside the district boundaries); or a

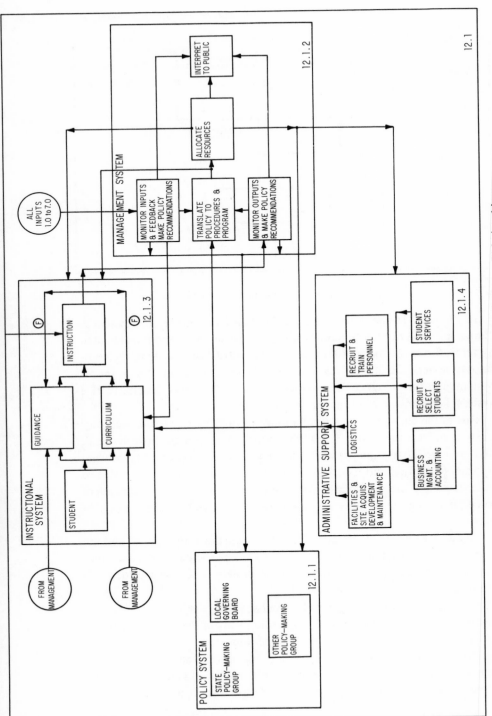

Figure 5-17.   The Model: Community College—Relationship of Functions, Inputs, and Outputs.

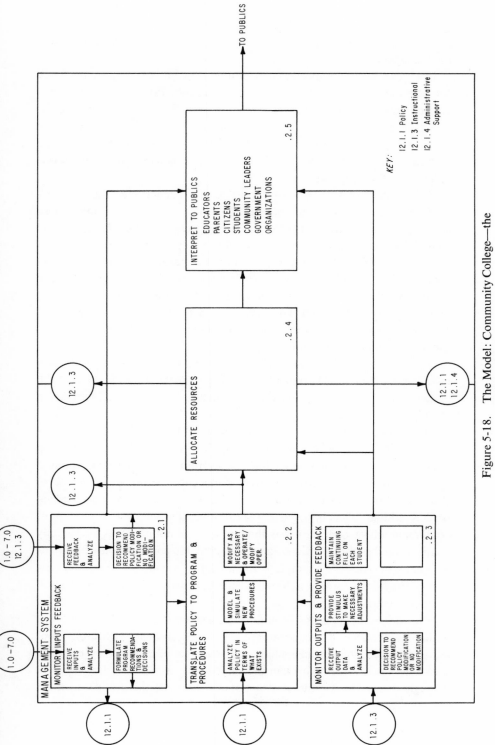

Figure 5-18. The Model: Community College—the Management System.

procedure or working relationship change between the policy system and the management system.

In Figure 5-18 an important task of management is to analyze feedback for purposes of making policy recommendations. For example, it is becoming apparent that no matter how a program in astrogeophysical technology is modified, the program cannot be operated in a cost-effective manner. It just isn't possible to purchase the laboratory equipment needed to cause students to meet the objectives. The policy recommendation: "phase out the program."

The product of the Monitor Inputs and Feedback element is policy recommendations, which are sent to the policy system for action. These are returned in the form of policy as "recommended," "modified," or "no change in existing policy." These policies, as appropriate, are translated into models simulating new procedures and "exercised" until the best configuration is achieved within existing constraints. It is often necessary to modify existing elements, information flows, and procedures in order to optimize the overall system. To insert a new element into an existing system does more than change its immediate surroundings. It alters in some way every element and aspect of the system.

After the model has been validated the new system is operationally tested and validated. The resources are then allocated on the basis of the policy translation and eventually the mobile units are built, data processing is added, and astrogeophysical technology is phased out.

The outputs of the system are monitored and analyzed in the same way as the inputs and translated where appropriate to policy recommendations.

A second, very critical, task that results from this analysis of output is system adjustment through resource reallocation within existing policy. Resources budgeted for a certain purpose are reallocated when feedback is received that this is necessary. For example, the purchase of an item of equipment whose operation was thought to be simulative was empirically demonstrated as the first few students reached this point to be ineffective as a simulation. Another example is the award of a contract to build a new unit of instruction, which is found by the first several students to reach it to be ineffectual.

A third major task of the Monitor Outputs and Provide Feedback block is the maintenance of a continuing file on each student. This file is contained in a data bank and includes as nearly as possible every response the student made during his tenure as a student, as well as follow-up data throughout his life. Besides instructional responses, there is data on his

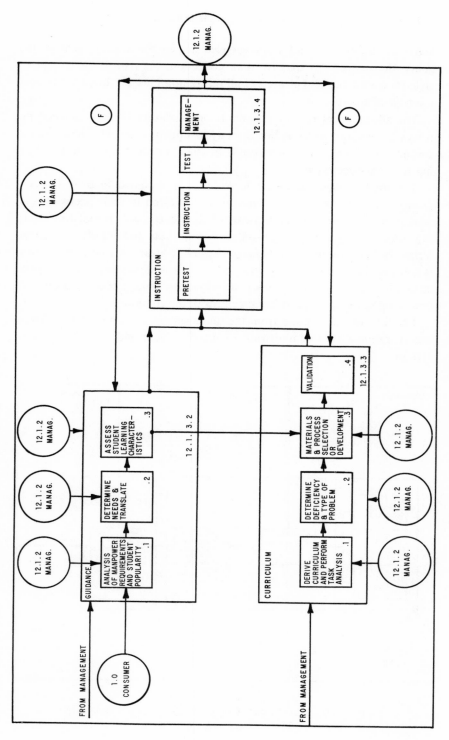

Figure 5-19. The Model: Community College—the Instructional System.

activities, dormitory, and whatever else helped the student achieve his goals. Because of this massive data collection, the data bank is kept in strictest confidence and cleared of all information not pertinent to the best interests of the student.

The allocation of resources is made on a priority basis as dictated by policy translation, which is tied directly to student learning. Therefore no resource is allocated unless it results in student performance, which then has to be demonstrated.

The final element, Interpret to Publics, is designed to provide each group in the community with information tailored to their needs. These various publics are to be made aware of all allocations of resources reflecting major policy changes, as well as the outputs and inputs in general terms. Its design is intended to make the public aware of where the money is going and how it is directly reflected in increased learning. Most importantly, it is evident that all types of individuals from the community are becoming measurably productive citizens of the community.

The flow of information from the management system serves to direct the operation of the administrative support system and the instructional system.

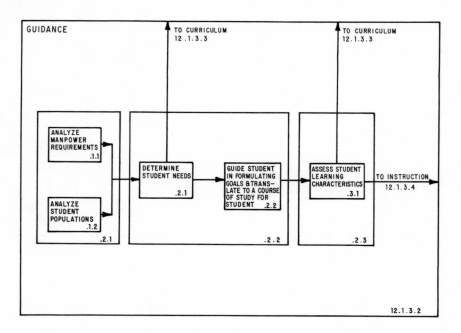

Figure 5-20. The Model: Community College—Guidance.

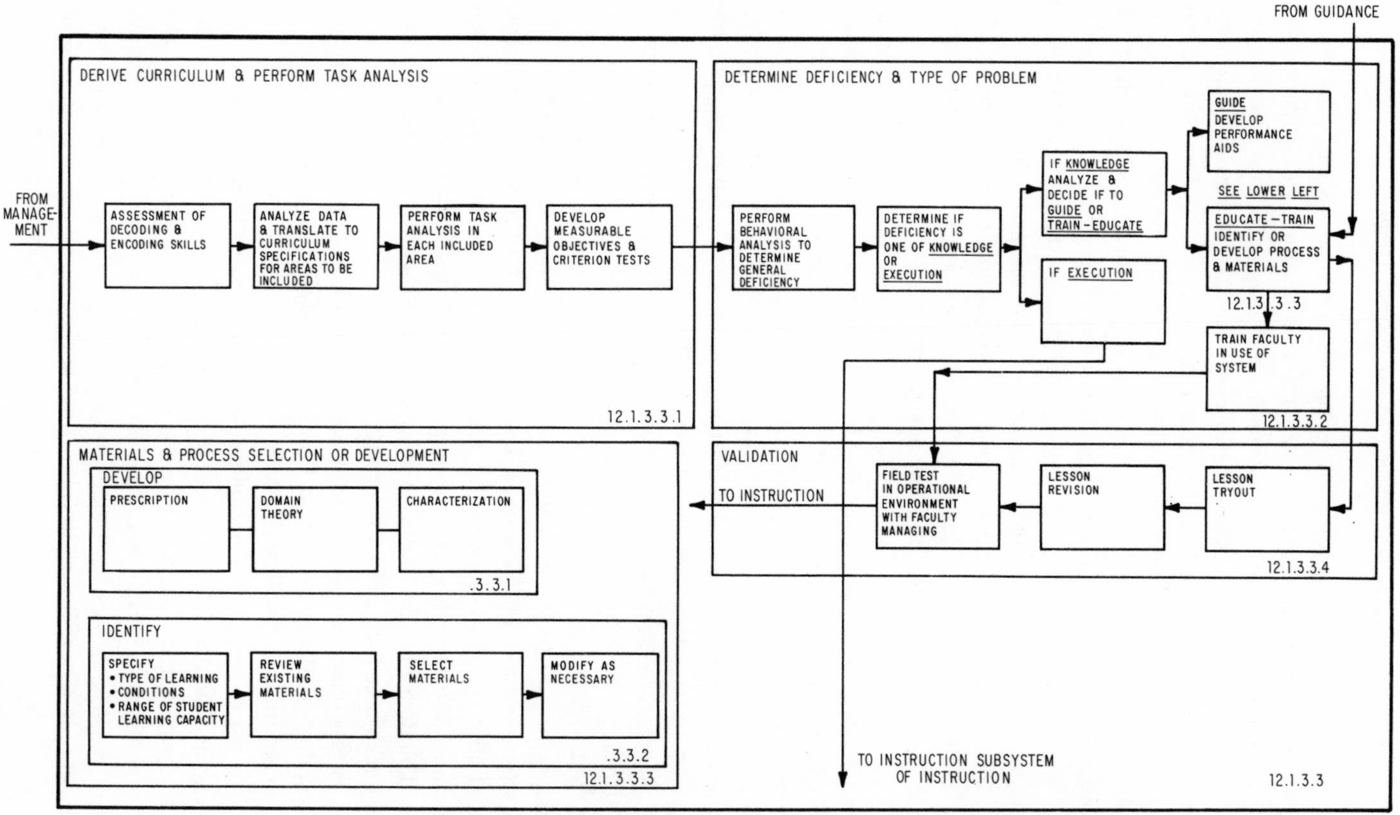

Figure 5-21. The Model: Community College—The Curriculum.

Figure 5-19 is a closer look at the instructional system. Observe the flow of information from the student to the curriculum and guidance functions, each of which will be analyzed further in later figures. The output of these two functions—"student learning characteristics profile and needs prescription" and "validated instructional processes"—form the primary information inputs to the instruction function. The instruction function's output is learning, or lack of it, and this important feedback is channeled back into the system to be used as data for modification.

Figures 5-20, 5-21, 5-22 represent graphically three major subsystems in the instructional system—guidance, curriculum, and instruction.

The student, as the input or object of instruction, comes to the learning experience with a set of learning characteristics. He is the central purpose for the existence of the instructional system.

The guidance function receives inputs from outside the system and relates them to student needs that have been assessed within this function. Student needs are compared with manpower requirements, the product of which is a plan of study formulated to help the student meet his goals. To insure that he does meet them, and in the most efficient manner possible, a careful assessment is made of learning characteristics. All of this data then passes to the instruction subsystem.

More activity goes on and more resources may be expended in the curriculum subsystem than in the others. The basic inputs are information about what the student needs to know and needs to be able to do; what it takes for him to learn all this; how relevance may be preserved so that inappropriate or obsolete skills, knowledges, and attitudes are not taught; and all necessary behaviors are acquired by the student. (A rationale and plan for the derivation of curriculum may be found in Chapter 3.)

The data thus derived is then translated into curriculum specifications for each area included by the policy system.

A *task analysis* is performed in each area to determine the encoding and decoding skill requirements. From this analysis, measurable objectives and criterion tests will be drafted.

In the second box a behavioral analysis is performed to establish the general deficiency of the student population. Next, a determination is made as to whether the deficiency is knowledge or execution: Has the student the skills and knowledge to function, but for one reason or another does not; or does he lack such skill and knowledge? If the problem is one of execution, that information is provided to the instruction subsystem as not solvable by training or education. This type of problem is frequently one of motivation and has to be solved by behavioral management.

If it is determined that the deficiency is knowledge- or skill-based, the decision must be made whether to guide the student by developing performance aids or to educate-train by identifying or developing the processes and materials.[64] If materials are to be used, existing materials and processes are reviewed first; only if they fail to meet the deficiency are new materials developed. The mathematical process is employed in developing learning experiences from the task analysis already performed, through prescription, domain theory, and characterization. As the materials are developed or identified, they are tested and revised until they reach an acceptable level of efficiency in bringing about student learning. When a prototype of the product is ready, the training of faculty and other personnel in the use of the product begins. Faculty training is completed before field testing.

Next, the materials identified or developed are put into a form usable in the instruction subsystem and field tested in the environment under management of the faculty who will ultimately use them. The learning processes developed must again reach an acceptable standard, for example, 90 percent of students with certain learning characteristics will meet the standard

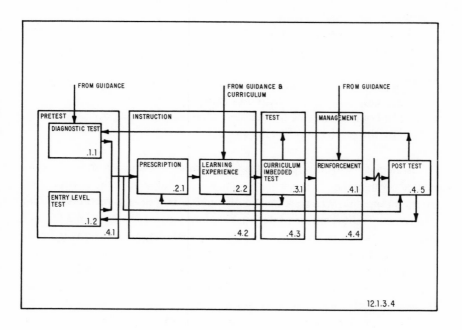

Figure 5-22.   The Model: Community College—Instruction.

set for each objective of the program. If the product fails this criterion, it will then be revised and tested again. This validation continues until the program meets the standard. Once validated, the learning strategy is ready for use in instruction.

The pretest developed in the curriculum and guidance subsystems is administered in the instruction subsystem. Based on the results of this test, a "prescription" is developed for each student tested. This prescription is written in the form of a contract and specifies the learning experiences with which the student is to interact and details what he is to learn in terms of skill, knowledge, or attitude and how each will be measured.

The student then goes through the validated learning process and is tested when he completes it. Learning is reinforced, nonlearning is not. If the student does not learn, a second diagnosis is made and the same or a different strategy is prescribed. If the student meets the standard set, the contract is consummated and a new prescription and contract is prepared. This process continues until the student reaches the end of a unit of instruction, at which point he is given the post-test.

Each step the student takes, each response he makes, is recorded and used to develop more adequate prescriptions for the student and as data to refine the learning processes.

The process described in the instructional model, while quite simplistic, is powerful in operation when rigorously followed. You must:

Specify what the student must do to demonstrate he has learned.
Develop strategies to help him learn.
Find out whether he has learned what was anticipated.
Use the results to refine the strategies.

Strategies, learning processes, or lessons—whatever they may be called—might have components which include: a hike in a wilderness area, a rappel down a rock face, a dialogue with a peer, a recorded oration by Winston Churchill or Malcolm X, a film loop of a "day in the life of a tiger lily," a visit to an art gallery, a scrambled text, a hand-scrawled note, or a dittoed sheet.

The measurement devices encompass the same range of vehicles, being tied as closely as possible to the "real" requirements. If one is attempting to test for performance of a telemark on a pair of skis or the removal of a rudder from a Boeing 707 or even completion of a federal income tax form taking advantage of all deductions, then one must measure the actual performance or a high simulation of such performance. A verbal description may not be substituted for actual performance unless the verbal description is the desired behavior. Therefore, in testing for encoding and decoding skills, such performance must occur in the "real" environment or in a high level simulation, such as those noted above.

6

An Experience in Employing a Systems Approach to a Community College

After studying the development of a single community college in some detail and comparing their experience with the experiences of other institutions attempting to use the "systems approach," I came to this conclusion: *No institution is truly employing a systems approach to either overall institutional development and operation or to instruction on an across-the-board basis.* My conclusion was also supported by Richard Wilson, now associate executive director of the American Association of Junior Colleges.[1]

In this chapter the development of the college is superimposed on the elements of the systems approach in order to show where deviations occurred. Then its operation is compared to its operation as if it were using the model developed in Chapter 5. Finally, an attempt is made to answer the question: Why was the systems approach not followed, what went wrong, not only at this college but at many institutions?

POINTS AT WHICH THE SYSTEMS APPROACH WAS NOT EMPLOYED

You will remember that the systems approach requires:

1. A clear description of goals and objectives.

2. A clear delineation of constraints.
3. The establishment of measures of effectiveness.
4. The synthesis of alternative solutions which consider all significant aspects of the problem.
5. The establishment of cost elements.
6. A cost-effectiveness analysis to establish trade-offs among solutions.
7. The continuing evaluation and feedback.

The basic question to be answered is, at which points in the development of its instructional program did the college deviate from the process outlined above? It should be emphasized that the elements above, though they may be combined or expanded, still represent the *essential* elements necessary in taking a "systems approach" to the problems of instruction.

1. *A Clear Description of Goals and Objectives*

The purposes, missions, and goals of the institution were well developed in written form. The translation of these goals into objectives was never brought to a criteria of measurability. The first year of the college's development saw a number of behavioral objectives developed for many of the courses offered during that year. It may be safe to estimate that as much as 50 percent of the objectives was completed for the courses. Not all of the objectives were completely measurable, but they at least represented some degree of measurability.

There is evidence that during the second and third years few objectives were drafted in behavioral terms. It was also noted that of those objectives drafted, nearly all were concerned with a description of behavior in the cognitive and psychomotor domains as defined by Benjamin Bloom.[2] I was unable to find a single objective reflecting behavior that could be classified in the affective domain, yet in conversations, many faculty members expressed concern for the importance of this area and said they wanted students to modify certain attitudes or shape their own value systems.

There was no evidence that measurable objectives were used in the management of the instructional program or its support systems. In other words, there was no pre-specification as to what would be acceptable as evidence that a problem had been resolved or a standard achieved. There were instances where criteria were specified in advance in other areas of management, for example, in the selection of sites and development of facilities. It was particularly interesting that in the area of finances and business administration, criteria were not established until there was a major crisis.

2. *A Clear Delineation of Constraints*

In approaching the problem of instruction after specification of objectives, the conditions and parameters of the problem must be delimited. If some students are reading at a 5.0 vocabulary level, with 75 percent comprehension at 75 words per minute, it should be known to the instructor. It is not good or bad, just a fact that must be considered. Likewise, it should be known when a student possesses the knowledge or skill to be learned before instruction.

There is evidence that in many programs no assessment was made of the learner prior to instruction. This assessment should include student learning characteristics; the skills, knowledge, and attitudes the student is expected to have as prerequisites or the skills, knowledge, and attitudes he is supposed to have acquired as a result of instruction.

At the support level, time, material, and other resource constraints were not realistically or clearly specified. Imposed by human resources, both in time and expertise, the constraints were not systematically described and considered.

In summary, there were few instances where the range of constraints bearing on any given situation were systematically delimited. A notable exception to this generalization was related to me by a faculty member; it concerned a reading class in which student characteristics were systematically assessed, resource and human constraints delimited, and a program instituted within these known constraints. There were certainly other instances, but they were exceptions rather than the rule.

3. *The Establishment of Measures of Effectiveness*

Measures of effectiveness represent what will be acceptable as evidence that objectives have been achieved. In instruction, these are the criterion tests; in the management of an institution, they are evidences that will be accepted in deciding whether criteria or standards have been met—objectives attained and goals reached.

At the instructional level the faculty, in some instances, produced rather complete instruments to measure attainment of the objectives. In most instances, however, this was not accomplished. Tests were devised in all courses, but when these tests are compared to the objectives as stated, it becomes evident that something was lost in the translation.

At the management level there was little indication that this evidence of movement toward or attainment of an objective was ever specified with regard to the instructional program.

In the overall management of the site-selection process and to a limited degree in facilities development, there was evidence of this establishment of measures of effectiveness.

4. *The Synthesis of Alternate Solutions Which Considers All Significant Aspects of the Problem*

The solutions, in the context of instruction, relate to message design, media configuration, and instrumentation alternatives. Consideration is also given to organization alternatives: large group, small group, independent study, or laboratory experience. The type of experience—field trip, role-playing, lecture, actual participation, or other—should also be considered.

Solutions, in the context of management, consider the various possible allocations of resources (human and materiel), as well as organizational and administrative considerations that are possible within the constraints.

There is little evidence that this element was exercised in the instructional program at the college, other than in isolated instances, at either instructional or management level. At the management level, alternate solutions were synthesized preliminary to the selection of a site and in the development of facilities.

5. *The Establishment of Cost Elements*

In this step each alternative solution is costed. These costs include initial outlays amortized over the useful life of the product or service. This is done to provide a basis for comparison.

I found no evidence that this costing was accomplished to more than a very limited degree except in one or two isolated instances. This is not to say that existing and proposed programs were not costed, but that the detailed costing of various instructional strategies was not evident.

At the management level, in the selection and development of site and facilities, this step was taken, but in most other areas I found little evidence of the costing.

6. *A Cost-Effectiveness Analysis to Establish Trade-Offs Among Solutions*

Which solution will produce the best conditions of learning for the student so that he will meet the objectives with the least expenditure of resources—the least cost? The idea is to get the most student learning for the limited resources available.

If any of the first five elements were ignored in the process, this step could not be taken. I encountered no instance in the instructional program of the college where this was systematically accomplished. At the management level this type of analysis was effected for site and facilities development, although I found no evidence of the information being related in any way to student learning.

7. *The Continuing Evaluation and Feedback*

This *essential* element provides for the continuing evaluation of the system, and when found lacking, the revision of it after it is implemented. You will recall that this iterative process of test-revise-test-revise-test . . . until the objectives are met is termed *validation* and is a continuing process.

In instruction, if the qualified student, after completing the instructional prescription, does not meet the objectives, the system is revised. That is, the prescription, materials, processes, or whatever is modified.

There was no evidence of this step being carried out in either the instructional or management areas in support of instruction.

Operation of the College in Relation to the Model

It is suggested that the reader turn to the reprint of the graphic portion of the model (Figs. 5-15 through 5-22), pages 175-180 to follow in reading this section.

Figure 5-15. Inputs to Community College from Other Systems

The college has developed both formally and informally some of these flows of information and lines of communication with the outside.

The *community* (2.0) has been connected through citizens committees, advisory committees, and in certain other, less formal, ways.

The *consumers* (1.0) have not been connected formally to the college through graduate follow-ups or other feedback mechanisms. There have been some informal connections through various individual staff members meeting informally with some graduates.

The *educational institutions* (3.0) have been only loosely connected to the college for information. The colleges and universities to which the college sends graduates, and the high schools from which it receives students, are both sources of vital information. The lines to the high schools have been strengthened substantially since the beginning of the college.

The lines of communication to *organizations* (4.0), such as unions, trade associations, guilds, and numerous others, are quite loose. There was little evidence that these lines were being utilized in any formal way, but there were indications that some had been established prior to and during the first year of the college's operation.

The *government* (5.0) lines to the state and national levels are in place, but the evidence shows little utilization at the federal level. The communications line to the state seems to be well established.

The lines to receive inputs from the *supporting technologies* (6.0) or the *disciplines* (7.0) are only loosely established and in the case of many of the technologies, are nonexistent.

Figures 5-16 and 5-17. Community College

The four systems as illustrated in Figure 5-16, which form the community college, are the Policy System (12.1.1), Management System (12.1.2), Instructional System (12.1.3), and Administrative Support System (12.1.4).

During the three years the college has been in operation, the interrelationships and information flows have changed rather substantially from time to time. The principal changes have occurred in the relationships of the policy system to the other systems. In the model in Figure 5-16, the policy system is connected only to the management system where a line providing for a two-way flow of information is illustrated. There is evidence that at various times in the college's development the policy system assumed management prerogatives and connected itself directly to the administrative support system in a two-way flow and to the instructional system in a one-way flow. The information lines that existed from the outside coming into the management system were at times diverted to the policy system. This occurred when governing committee members assumed administrative prerogatives through the business office. Likewise, during the first year of operation the direction of the instructional program was in one or more instances undertaken by the governing committee.

Present information-flow relationships exist as illustrated in the model and are becoming stabilized. This is not to imply that the information needs of the college are being met, but merely that the lines do exist. The present college administration recognized the need for communication and has identified it as a key problem. Recently intra- and intercampus information flows have been tightened by frequent meetings, tele-conferences, and written documentation between personnel at all levels in the college.

Figure 5-18. Management System (12.1.2)

The management system of the college is not formally established with these functional relationships, thus making comparison difficult.

The president, president's council, vice-president, and business manager form the management team. All major administrative and management decisions are developed cooperatively.

Inputs and outputs of the system are not formally monitored.

Resources are not allocated strictly in support of the instructional system based on feedback, nor are they allocated based on the procedural model-building and exercise specified in the model.

Figure 5-19. Instructional System

The model shows three elements within the Instructional System: Guidance (12.1.3.2), Curriculum (12.1.3.3), and Instruction (12.1.3.4). The raw material that this system receives is students; the finished products are learned students—graduates.

Figure 5-20. Guidance

The guidance functions as illustrated in the model are not evident in the college. The college has expressed a general need in this area. Therefore the information flow to and feedback from the instruction element is nearly nonexistent in the college.

Figure 5-21. Instruction

The tasks to be performed in the *Instruction* block as illustrated, include pretesting, instructing, testing, and managing the operation.

While certain courses in the college are employing this model, the majority are not, although this model is the same as the college's original model.

The feedback flows, from the product of *Instruction* to *Guidance* and *Curriculum*, are not established within the college's instructional system.

Figure 5-22. Curriculum

The curriculum block, although quite well developed in the original college model, has fallen into disuse, due principally to a lack of definition between the curriculum function and the instruction function. The present college model combines the functions specified within curriculum with those in instruction and neither are clearly delineated.

It is apparent from this cursory inspection of the *relationship* between the model and the operation of the college that within the channels that do exist, different information is being transmitted than that which was envisioned in the model. However, it is also evident that the college's model bears little relationship to the model as developed here.

EXPERIENCES OF OTHER INSTITUTIONS

The principal problems encountered in other institutions seems to be similar to those encountered at the community college. The core of their problems seems to lie with a basic misunderstanding of what the systems approach is, and the preoccupation with methodology. The problem may be even more basic than this and may lie with education's fascination with artifacts and disregard for the underlying process.

Whatever the reasons, this attention to tools and methodologies at the expense of the process has produced several major problems in nearly every institution attempting to exercise a systems approach to the problems of instruction. The problems are:

1. A confusion between the functions of *curriculum* and those of *instruction* has resulted in many institutions ignoring the real requirements because "the instructor doesn't have the time."
2. The lack of attention to the product—the student. Few institutions make any real provision for quality control because little is known about whether the student met the objectives. This may be due to the fact that few courses are really developed on the basis of meas-

urably stated objectives, the attainment of which is adequately measured by criterion-referenced tests.

3. Closely allied with the above is the problem of using this knowledge about how well the student did in relation to the objectives to improve the system. Feedback elements are rarely in evidence.

Many other problems could be cited, but these, in my opinion, were the most critical. If solved, they would allow the process to operate. This, in turn, would provide the mechanism necessary for handling the other problems and setting in motion the iterative process that produces movement toward a goal by successive approximation.

SUMMARY

The college studied is one of the most innovative institutions in the complex of community and junior colleges in the nation. The president, a nationally known educator and highly competent administrator, has developed a staff and faculty whose competence and dedication have been pointed to by nearly every educator visiting the institution and by the several accrediting association consultants. The governing board's dedication is obvious from the thousands of hours of freely given time they spent in building the institution. I frankly found no institution that had accomplished more in individualizing instruction for the student.

Although the college takes pride in its learner-center philosophy—the greatest strength of the college is in its commitment to a learner-oriented philosophy and the resultant subordination of all other traditional college concerns to this commitment—the evidence of implementation is not apparent. First, a "learner-centered" instructional plan was to be achieved through application of the instructional systems approach to the learning process, which demanded "predetermined behavioral objectives. . . ." These have not been drafted in all courses. Second, if student needs are truly to be met, then data on student progress, in terms of predetermined behavioral objectives, must not only be collected but used in two ways: the modification of future instructional prescriptions for the student to insure mastery, and as a basis for modifying the instructional materials and processes.

A real commitment to learning was not made by the college. For example, at no point did the governing board call for or receive a report on student progress, nor did they ever approve a resource allocation in a specific area to correct a measured deficiency in that program, as measured by what students had or had not learned. They failed to hold the president accountable for student learning, nor did the president hold his staff and faculty accountable.

The original instructional program of the college, although organized within a rather rigid audio-tutorial structure, was not based on measurable objectives (though many were written). Criterion tests were developed in some instances only. No usable assessment of student learning characteristics was made. The learning strategies that were developed, in most cases lacked the necessary structure and replicability to make them effective. And of paramount importance, no learning process was truly validated. Even in the most highly developed curricular areas, the data gathered as a result of students working through the programs and taking the post-tests is collecting dust in file folders.

There is hardly a component of the systems approach that was not violated. How is it possible that a highly competent administration and faculty, committed to the concept of individualizing instruction through exercising a systems approach, could permit this to happen, particularly when many of the administrators and some of the faculty had been involved previously with programs in other institutions that encountered similar difficulties?

The answer may be relatively simple in conceptualization when placed within the framework of the community college model developed here.

First, the college, although attempting to follow an instructional systems approach to its instructional program, became fixed on the "methodology" and *it* became labeled the "systems approach." To take a systems approach does not necessarily mean that you employ an audio-tutorial methodology, nor does it mean absence of lectures, commitment to audio-visual presentations, nor any of the other "artifacts" of instruction. It implies exactly what has been described as the systems approach—a procedure for processing problems.

A second major answer to the problem is that it is critical to use a systems approach to the solution of problems at all levels, not just instruction. This is true because a system, as a group of interrelated components pulling together toward a common goal, is an entity, an organic structure. It is more than the sum of its parts. In fact, the alteration of any single component produces changes in all other components. Therefore every element—instruction, guidance, and curriculum within the instructional subsystem, and every subsystem within the community college (instruction, management, policy, and administrative support)—must all be organized as an interrelated whole.

The administrative organization at the college did not support the instructional program optimally, as it lacked sensitivity to the support requirements. The meager resources available, therefore, were expended in less than optimal ways to maximize learning.

The very critical curriculum function described in the model did not really exist, since validated learning processes were supposed to be developed by faculty members with a full load in performing the instructional function.

Guidance was not well serviced and, as was mentioned before, assessments of student characteristics were never performed.

The community college I have described is in no way unique. The problems in employing the approach it has encountered have also been evident at other institutions which have attempted to employ the approach in various ways.

Individual faculty members, within their constraints, are doing some innovative things by traditional standards. Many of the faculty meet their courses in a modified audio-tutorial organizational pattern, some have developed instructional materials that are of high quality, and almost without exception they possess a degree of dedication that *far* exceeds the norm for college faculties.

7

Guidelines in Employing a Systems Approach

In this final chapter, the information I gathered during the study and other information collected in the course of its development are used to formulate a set of guidelines for a new institution to follow in developing its instructional program through the employment of a systems approach.

First, the nine principal findings of the study are listed; second, the systems approach as a process is described by an example of each element in the process; and third, suggestions are given as to how the findings may be applied to the development of an instructional program in a community college.

The graphic portion of the model developed in Chapter 5 has been reproduced for convenient reference on pages 175-180.

FINDINGS OF THE STUDY

Finding 1: Substantial evidence exists that technology will not dehumanize man. On the contrary, man is dependent on tools and technology for his humanity. The basic process of all technology is the systems approach.

Finding 2: Man must use technology to solve his problems. In doing so in education, he must develop lines of communication with the basic sciences and other areas of human knowledge so that this knowledge may be brought to bear on practical problems facing the field.

Finding 3: A theory of instruction, founded on two principles, is emerging:

> Man is a behavior-acquiring organism, therefore learning as a modification of behavior is man's natural state.
> A man's behavior is determined by his perception of the consequences of that behavior.

This emerging theory of instruction may be described as follows:

The human being is constantly seeking stimulation and modifying his behavior in an effort to control his environment. The direction and character of this modification is determined by his perceptions of the consequences of any unit, course, curriculum, or other learning experience. Then, through the shaping of these perceptions, so that they more closely approximate reality, the learner is able to learn and to make intelligent choices.

Finding 4: The task of instruction is to prepare the learner for a lifetime of efficient learning in a dynamic environment by:

Specifying the outcomes in terms of his behavior.

Determining what the individual perceives as the consequences of the behavior.

Shaping his perceptions of these consequences to more nearly approximate reality.

Providing learning experiences that increase the encoding and decoding skill levels, thereby permitting him to employ increasingly complex symbolic systems. These skills will enable him to acquire efficiently ever more fulfilling behavior consistent with the philosophy stated in Finding 5.

Providing checks to determine that he is becoming more efficient and effective as a learner and modifying experiences as necessary based on this feedback.

Finding 5: All elements of education in a dynamic society founded on democratic ideals should:

Place the individual at the center of the system.

Prepare the individual to flourish in a dynamic society which requires constant modifications of his behavior.

Not impose the standards of the present society on any future generation.

Recognize the individual as an idiosyncratic learner who modifies his behavior based on his perceptions of the consequences.

Prepare and equip the individual for freedom.

Help develop the inborn capacity of love in each individual.

Finding 6: To increase the probability of success in achieving the goals and purposes of the institution, existing knowledge is applied through the medium of technology, using the systems approach at all levels. The essential elements of this approach are:

A clear description of goals and objectives.

A clear delineation of constraints.

The establishment of measures of effectiveness.

The synthesis of alternate solutions.

The establishment of cost elements.

A cost-effectiveness analysis to establish trade-offs among solutions.

Continuing evaluation and feedback.

Finding 7: The model of the community college instructional system produced shows:

Lines of external communication being established with seven areas of society—

(1.0) consumers

(2.0) community

(3.0) educational institutions

(4.0) organizations

(5.0) government

(6.0) supporting technology

(7.0) disciplines

Internal lines of communication depicted by arrows between the systems, subsystems, and elements.

Systems and subsystems and the functions that must be performed in each, and their interrelationships. Within the community college there are four major systems: *instructional, management, administrative support,* and *policy.* Within each system the following subsystems perform these activities:

instructional curriculum, guidance, instruction

management monitor inputs, monitor outputs, translate policy into procedure and programs, allocate resources, interpret to publics

administrative support system facilities and site acquisition, development, and maintenance; logistics; recruit and train personnel; business management and accounting; recruit and select students; student services administration

policy local governing board (acting on policy recommendations), state policy-making group (formulating regulations), other policy-making groups (legislation)

Instructional system: The tasks that must be performed in the instructional system are:

curriculum

- derive curriculum (assess educational skills, analyze data and translate it into curriculum specifications, perform task analyses, develop objectives and criterion tests)
- determine deficiency and type of problem: perform behavioral analysis to determine general deficiency; determine if deficiency is one of knowledge or execution; if execution, pass to instruction; if knowledge, determine if to guide or educate-train; if guide, develop performance aids; if educate-train, identify or develop process and materials and train faculty; validate[1]

The product of curriculum is a validated instructional process ready for use in instruction.

guidance

- analyze student population and manpower requirements
- determine student needs; guide student in formulating goals and translate to course of study for student
- assess student learning characteristics

The product of guidance is information on the above, which is provided to instruction.

instruction
- pretest
- instruct
- test
- manage

The product is a student equipped to meet his objectives.

Finding 8: It was discovered that institutions purportedly employing the systems approach to their programs are not succeeding. Most employ some of the artifacts and some of the elements in the process. I found a problem common to many programs in their lack of adaptiveness to meet stated purposes. Adaptiveness is not really a question of *if*, but rather a question of *how*. An institution whose purpose is to meet the educational needs of its community has three alternatives. It may *adapt reactively* to pressure from the community, *compromise its purposes*, or *systematically adjust* the system *as signals are received* through communications channels. The core of this problem seems to lie in the institution's failure to establish these three elements: (1) lines of communication to the community (the seven segments noted in the model) and within the institution, (2) specification of information to be transmitted, (3) processing of information and resultant system adjustment. Even in cases where substantial information is collected, it is not put to use.

Finding 9: Development of a management and an administrative support system that is supportive of the instructional system is critical to realization of the purpose of the community college.

THE SYSTEMS APPROACH AS A PROCESS

Most colleges that are sincerely interested in assuming the responsibility for identifying and meeting the educational needs of the community via the systems approach run into difficulty by failing to differentiate between "things" and the process. Tape recorders and tape may be purchased and put in an audio laboratory, or a remote access information retrieval system may be installed, where the student may dial for a particular audio tape. Computer assisted instruction may be implemented. But these are artifacts—they are not the systems approach. All kinds of software may be developed or purchased and learning laboratories and resource centers may be opened around the clock. It could be made a crime for an instructor to give a lecture and still not have a systems approach. Behavioral objectives and criterion tests could be written, alternative, multimedia strategies developed for each objective, and still not utilize the approach. *These are the things, the artifacts of instruction.*

The systems approach is nothing more nor less than a procedure for handling problems.

A systems approach demands:

A clear definition of goals and objectives.

A delineation of constraints.

A description of measures of effectiveness.

Synthesis of alternate solutions.

Establishment of cost elements.

Cost-effectiveness analysis to establish trade-offs among solutions.

Continuing evaluation and feedback.

These procedures may be combined or subdivided, but they are the essential elements of the approach.

Second, the systems approach is a process; it is nothing in and of itself until it has a problem to process. Then it becomes a set of guidelines which help to bring all possible information to bear on a problem. So organized, it is set up for solution, test of solution and revision until the problem-solver is satisfied with the solution; that is, it achieves the standards quantitatively and qualitatively with the least possible resource expenditure.

In order to better understand the process as it may apply to a community college, examples of each element are provided on the following pages. Assume that you are a president of a community college as you study the examples.

1. A Clear Definition of Goals and Objectives

Example 1:

Many students entering your college do not read as well as you think they should, so you set an objective: All students graduating from this institution will read at least to the following standard: 7.0 vocabulary, 90 percent comprehension at 300 words per minute on nontechnical material.

Example 2:

In your college's statement of philosophy it says, students are to be able

to "make worthy use of their leisure time." This has been variously interpreted by curriculum committees as making sure that the student is
equipped with a wide repertory of leisure skills (recreational, aesthetic,
etc.), a personal commitment and the skills and knowledges necessary to
perform community services, and the skills and knowledges necessary for
independent learning. You and your curriculum committee have recommended and the board has approved the following statement:

> In order to be able to make worthy use of leisure time, a student grad-
> uating from this institution will have: (1) demonstrated a level of pro-
> ficiency in a minimum of ten recreational or vocational areas; the level
> of proficiency will be prescribed for each activity and will be dictated
> by the level of skill necessary to "enjoy" the game or activity. (The
> master of each area will establish the level in measurable written terms.)
> (2) participated in some manner in at least two community service
> projects which may include any of the following: work in community,
> health, civic, or other organizations; help in schools, libraries, or other
> institutions; or participation in community services such as drives,
> special days, or other activities.

You decided that "learning how to learn" is really the overall objective
of the total program and that the sum of the objectives in all areas must
lead to this. Therefore you have elected not to specify this under "worthy
use of leisure time."

Example 3:

One of the objectives you may have for faculty members is the drafting
of sub-objectives to measure progress toward these terminal objectives.

> Faculty members, given a goal of the institution stated as a terminal
> objective, will develop or select the interim objectives that will measure
> progress toward mastery.

You may consider the above examples of objectives to be rather pedes-
trian or may not agree with them. Remember that we are only interested
in demonstrating and learning to use the process. You may develop whatever objectives are necessary based on the goals of your institution when
you actually do it.

Let us now look at a way to begin drafting objectives. Even before attempting to define problems in the traditional sense, it is helpful to specify

what you'll accept as evidence that the problem is solved. Here are some examples:

When our students no longer cut classes, the problem is solved. Right now, I'll accept 90 percent attendance.

When less than 1 percent of our graduates who transfer to colleges and universities, fail or drop out of school, our problem is solved.

When our student body numbers 1,000. . . .

The above evidence of problem solution has one thing in common—it is all measurable. We know when it happens.

Let's look at other examples that are less management- and more instruction-oriented:

When the student can draw a great circle route on a mercator projection without deviating more than 1° at any point on the route.

When the student can execute christies in sequence on a 20° packed slope in 60 seconds or less without moving his skiis or ankles more than 3 inches apart at any time, while staying in the fall line of the slope.

When the student can take a patient's blood pressure so that the systolic and diastolic counts do not vary more than two points from that taken by a master nurse on the same patient.

When the student is able to isolate the five elements in a chemical solution, knowing the volume of water and of one chemical.

When after listening to Uninsky, Rubenstein, and Van Cliburn perform five Chopin etudes, the student will be able to identify the musician in each case.

These objectives, which describe the evidence that will be accepted as proof that the problem is solved, are critical to the systems approach. The *Talmud* remains the source of wisdom here for the nonbeliever: "If you don't know where you're going, then any road will get you there."

Let us look at the various ways we use objectives. They are important because they:

Provide a basis for deciding what measures are needed to accomplish them.

Help us to decide which of several ways of achieving our goals is the "best way," that is, which solution gives us the most effective performances at the least cost.

Provide a basis for evaluating the performance of our solution after we have implemented it: Did it work or do we have to revise and try again?

A word of caution: when you initially specify objectives for a system, you may not know whether these objectives are technically or economically feasible within the constraints. Later on, in the analysis process, you may find that your original objectives cannot be met by any of the potential solutions that are within the amount of money you have been given. It then becomes necessary to modify your original objectives based on the facts of your analysis. The systems approach is necessarily iterative, that is, the process repeats itself until by successive approximation a realistic, workable set of objectives and solutions is evolved. Hence your initial set of objectives may contain a number of "nice to have" objectives, which may have to be compromised later or dropped, depending on the facts of your analysis.

In generating objectives, be sensible. Don't get "hung up" at the beginning by trying to decide on the detailed technical and economic feasibility of an objective. You will have an opportunity to modify the objectives based on more factual data later in the design process, should they prove unrealistic.

2. A Clear Delineation of Constraints

Obviously we have to operate in a real world, a world that already exists and is relatively slow to change; a world that makes certain facilities and resources available to us and denies us others; a world that has administrative problems, time constraints, monetary constraints, physical and legal laws within which we must operate in devising possible solutions to the problem of meeting our objectives. Defining these constraints and making them explicit is an essential step in determining possible solutions. These are the *conditions* we must "live within" in trying to accomplish our objective.

Constraints are sometimes construed as negative since they seem to block what we want to do. They are not negative but merely represent reality. They make explicit the bounds within which we must operate. The fact that you have 500 boys and 500 girls on your campus is a constraint. A declining assessed valuation of your district with a stabilized mill levy, a large industrial complex in your area with heavy training requirements, ten freshman students who are functional illiterates—these are all constraints.

A word of caution: constraints should be carefully analyzed to determine that they are not really variables. For many years a fixed schedule was viewed as a constraint in high schools when, in reality, it was a variable and did not need to set bounds on the instructional program. Likewise, many cherished constraints at the community college level may very well prove to be variables—variable entry, pacing and exit of students, often viewed as constraints, are under our control and therefore variables.

3. The Establishment of Measures of Effectiveness

You will remember that in stating objectives, evidence of problem solution was required. Now we must collect that evidence by constructing a measurement device that will measure whether or not the objectives have been met or the degree to which they were met.

The measure of effectiveness for an instructional system is student performance. This is measured by developing criterion-referenced tests to measure attainment or degree of attainment of the objectives.

Example 1:

Let's look for a moment at the objective we stated in Reading:

> . . . will read at least to the following standard—7.0 vocabulary, 90 percent comprehension at 300 words per minute on nontechnical material.

Our task is to develop a test that will measure attainment of this objective. Since criterion-measurement devices have already been produced and are being marketed, we select one that will measure attainment of the objective. The test we decide to use is the one of the standardized reading tests.

Example 2:

It is obvious when we look at Example 2 on page 151, that this objective will require that we construct rather than "pull off the shelf" some sort of measurement device. How do we measure the fact that a student has acquired a level of proficiency in certain recreational areas? How do we determine, for example, that a student can play a game of tennis? The answer is obviously, "Have him play a game." But what about the proficiency level; how well must he play the game? He must be able to serve; so let us first test his service. We give him six balls and draw a circle eight feet in diameter in the opposite service area. Tell him that he has two minutes to serve the six balls, and must place five of the six balls within the circle, to meet the criterion. Next, in order to play tennis well enough to "enjoy" it, he must be able to volley, so we specify that, after returning a serve, he must volley for a period of 15 seconds with an opponent of about equal skill. Finally, we would want the student to score and play by the rules of the game. To measure these latter behaviors, we have the student score a game and observe in a game situation that he plays by the rules by developing a check sheet and observing his performance. Please note that the student did *not* have to respond to a paper and pencil test on the rules since we wanted to determine whether he "played" by the rules, *not* whether he "knew" the rules. This is a common error in establishing measures of effectiveness.

Let's look at another example. Our objective is to have the student remove the heads on a V-8 engine and reseat them. We want him actually to perform the various operations involved, yet we ask him to tell us either orally or on paper what he would do. This is inappropriate and will not tell us whether the student can remove and reseat a head. We must measure his actual performance and may not substitute a paper and pencil test as a measure of effectiveness unless that is the objective.

In management situations, measures of effectiveness must be described just as explicitly. They consist of the prescription of what will constitute acceptability in quality and/or quantity of the product of an element in the system. For example, information received from employers of last year's graduates indicate that 50 percent held their jobs less than six months. In terms of the college's objectives, what does this mean? Is this acceptable performance or should the program be modified, and if so, how? All of this would have been answered by establishing measures of effectiveness in advance. We might arbitrarily have said that anything more than a 10 percent change in the first year should be investigated in the following manner:

1. A survey should have been made of all the graduates, both those who changed jobs and those who did not, in an effort to isolate the significant variables.
2. Once identified, these findings would be used as a basis for modification in the system.

At the same time, management should initiate a research effort to establish what constitutes an acceptable frequency of job change in first-year graduates, or if this is even an appropriate criterion. As you can see, this figure is variable and not a static consideration. All such standards, like a 7.0 reading level, are subject to modification based on evidence of a change in requirements. A reading level of 7.0 at 300 wpm may have been based on reading newspapers that are written at this vocabulary level. Perhaps this will change in the future, even to the point where reading, except as an artifact of a prior time, may be replaced with compressed speech and visuals as the principal vehicle of mass communication. Measures of effectiveness must be developed based on such objectives to permit this sort of modification, which is based on the feedback.

Measures of effectiveness then specify how the accomplishment of the objective is to be measured.

4. Synthesis of Alternate Solutions

After the measures of effectiveness have been developed, alternative solutions may be explored. This consists of formulating different ways of achieving objectives within the constraints identified after considering all aspects of the problem. Each solution synthesized must consider design, operation, testing, revision, and other management responsibilities, including changes in present policy, procedures, and resource allocations. Elements of different solutions may be the same, since totally "new" solutions are seldom synthesized.

In instruction, alternate solutions lie in many areas: different instructional strategies and the components within such strategies; message design, mediation and instrumentation; prescription of certain strategies for students with certain learning characteristics; and many others.

Example 1:

In servicing our objective that all students be able to read 7.0 material at 300 wpm with 90 percent comprehension, what are the alternatives within our constraints, considering that the attainment of the objective will be measured by a standardized reading test?

To build a new program from scratch, based on the learning characteristics of the students, would require more resources than we have. Resources do exist to measure the learning characteristics of the student body, since this is determined to be necessary for all courses. Let's look at two alternatives (realistically, we actually may wish to develop four or five):

Alternative #1

Pretest students to determine reading deficiency (difference between where each student is and the standard of 7.0, 300 wpm, 90 percent comprehension).

Instruct using off-the-shelf materials already available at college and treating students in group situation.

Post-test with standardized reading test to determine extent of deficiency remaining.

Alternative #2

Pretest, as above.

Instruct using off-the-shelf materials and purchasing of high-interest, low-vocabulary materials and SRA reading kits.

Post-test, as above.

5. The Establishment of Cost Elements

The purpose of this step is to cost each alternative solution. In calculating cost, we are interested in all costs amortized over the useful life of the material, equipment, or whatever; the pro rata cost of specialized personnel and facilities overhead; and the costs of training and other expenses attributable to the alternative.

6. A Cost Effectiveness Analysis

A cost versus effectiveness analysis is made so that we may make trade-off decisions between the alternate solutions. We are faced with the decision as to which of the alternative solutions creates the best conditions of learning for the student at the least cost. Since dollars are always limited and our business is to produce learning, we want to produce the most learning possible with the dollars available. We do not compromise our objectives, as this would be false economy; rather, we spend our money in the most effective manner possible, compromising objectives only as a last resort with full knowledge of what is being done.

If you look at Table 7-1, which compares the costs of the two alternatives, it is apparent that Alternative #1 is more costly. This is due to a higher proportion of instructor time to paraprofessional time being used. Alternative #2 uses the paraprofessional for all nonprofessional tasks.

Software costs include the costs of all materials, including both consumable and nonconsumable materials. Nonconsumable material costs are calculated on the basis of their useful life with a pro rata proportion being charged for each usage.

Hardware costs include purchase, maintenance, and operating costs not included in "indirect costs"; calculation is made as with software on a per-use basis. For example, let's say the useful life of a cassette tape recorder is 5,000 hours and its original purchase price was $50; maintenance runs about $50 over the 5,000 hours of operation and there are no operating costs. The cost per hour of this machine, then, is $.02. The cost of a remote-access information retrieval system such as dial access, would be calculated in the same way, figuring machine maintenance and supervision time as a part of maintenance and operating costs.

Table 7-1.   Sample Cost Comparison of Two Instructional Strategies.

	Software Costs/ Student	Hardware Costs/ Student	Personnel Costs/ Student	Indirect Costs/ Student	Totals
Pretest					
Alternative #1	.10	—	.50	.05	.65
Alternative #2	.10	—	.50	.05	.65
Instruction					
Alternative #1	.25	—	1.50	.15	1.90
Alternative #2	.50	—	.50	.15	1.15
Post-test					
Alternative #1	.10	—	.50	.05	.65
Alternative #2	.10	—	.50	.05	.65
Totals					
Alternative #1	.45	—	2.50	.25	3.20
Alternative #2	.70	—	1.50	.25	2.45

Personnel costs include instructors, paraprofessionals, clerks, or others involved with the instruction. For example, is it always necessary to require an instructor whose time may cost $8-10 per hour to administer and score a pretest or post-test in preparation for professional diagnosis and prescription when this may be done by a clerk at $2.50 per hour? Activities such as an hour's lecture are costly in terms of instructor time. Whenever possible, save this valuable commodity for professional activities: diagnosis of where the student is in terms of what he wants to learn; prescription of an experience from which he will learn; and checking by reviewing the results of the test (not giving and scoring it). To have poor, nonvalidated instructional materials is false economy, because it will take additional professional level time to make up for the deficiency, if it can be done at all.

Costs may run high in this category unless cognizance is taken of the factors mentioned.

Indirect costs include a pro rata share of the depreciation, operation, and maintenance on any facility used; the pro rata cost of all management, guidance and support services of the college. Special requirements such as heavy use of electricity, gas, telephone, or other utilities would require increases over the fixed amount per unit of utilization.

To briefly summarize, the idea is to get the required learning for the least cost and be able to recognize when the learning is being compromised.

7. Continuing Evaluation and Feedback

The solution is tested to determine if it is effective, if it meets the objective. If it does not, then the solution is modified, based on the results that are fed back into the system. This is accomplished on a continuing basis with all system modification based on this feedback.

Let's look at our example again. When we test our solution (Alternative #2), we find that of the 100 students needing to upgrade their reading skills in terms of the standard, 25 did not make it. On close examination of the results it was found that 10 have reading disabilities requiring specialized equipment which the college doesn't have. The other 15 had a random assortment of deficiencies that appeared to reflect a lack of motivation.

The specialized equipment and materials necessary for the 10 students could be (a) purchase for $4,000, (b) rent for $300/month, or (c) the students could be sent to a reading clinic at a cost of $10 per month per student. You would calculate *all* costs for each alternative as before, make trade-offs, and reach a decision.

The motivational problem common to the 15 students might well be handled by increasing the range of reinforcers available to the instructor; providing support by getting specialized services to identify the reinforcers that each of the 15 will respond to—for example, "what behavior has a higher probability of occurrence than reading?" Another alternative may lie in identifying or developing, if not available, "off-the-shelf" materials of more interest to each of these 15, which may prove to be a part of the first alternative.

Once more, each alternative is costed, trade-offs made, and the new solution tried. Eventually we develop a solution that meets the standard for the least expenditure of resources within the constraints. You've got to be a little bull-headed and not give up before the standards you've set are reached.

You may be saying by now that all of this is too costly, we have too much to cover, too much to do, and just not enough time or money to employ this "systems approach." If you are short on time, money, and personnel and long on students, requirements, and demands, then *you can't afford not to use the systems approach*. This approach forces us to face our problems for what they are and helps us to devise a workable solution to them. We always know where we stand when we employ the process, and so does everyone else.

The approach is no panacea, but in competent hands it is a powerful tool.

Employing a Systems Approach to the Development of Your College

The systems approach, as you can see, is deceptively simple in conceptualization. It is easy to be seduced by the it's-nothing-but-common-sense group into believing that it is somehow a magical formula for success in all human endeavors. I hope that this myth has been dispelled. The process is rigorous, demanding a high level of discipline. In order to really get a feeling for the process you have to use it.

1. Attack the overall problem by solving a small problem facing you today, using this approach. This will give you a feel for the process.
2. Make it a point to explain the process to someone else after you've tried it. Then take another problem and try it again, modifying your technique where you had difficulty in the first problem.

After you become familiar with the process, it doesn't much matter where you start. Most descriptions of a systems approach start with a specification of goals and objectives. While general goal statements are easily specified (perhaps because they don't say anything), they seldom carry much meaning for instruction. To translate these goal statements into measurable objectives is quite another matter, and this is where many great hopes founder. These steps, however, can and must be accomplished.

Let's take a statement of purpose which most community colleges would accept and see how we might accomplish that purpose. The purpose of a community college is to serve the educational needs of all persons in the community, both youths and adults.[1]

If this purpose is carefully analyzed, it might be said that the community college is *of, by,* and *for* the community. The community is the only reason it exists. Its student body are members of the community, not just the young or unskilled, but *all,* since all people have educational needs. In this view, community members and student body become synonomous terms.

Since we are unique, dynamic creatures who are constantly learning those things we perceive to be self-satisfying in consequences, a problem arises. The range of needs is great and is in a continual state of flux. Therefore we must recognize that in order to help the individual meet his educational needs, we should equip him with the "educational skills" needed to learn whatever he perceives as being important to him. Our task, then, becomes one of helping the learner to learn efficiently and effectively.

This is accomplished through the development of experiences based on the following:

> The human being is constantly seeking stimulation and modifying his behavior in an effort to control his environment. The direction and character of this modification is determined by his perceptions of the consequences of his behavior. In order to assist or shape growth in a person it is necessary to determine his perceptions of the consequences of any unit, course, curriculum, or other learning experiences. Then through the shaping of these perceptions so that they more closely approximate reality, the learner is able to learn and to make intelligent choices.

It really doesn't matter where we start applying a systems approach after we have established our purpose, so let's start by setting up the communication, information, and management system to serve the college, which will make it possible to:

1. Identify educational needs on a continuing basis, since the college, to fulfill its purpose, must be responsive to the changing needs of the community members.
2. Translate these needs into a statement of the problem in terms of acceptable evidence that the problem is solved (an objective). In establishing this criteria, controls need to be established so that if the needs are being met (as measured by the criteria established) no adjustment would be necessary, but if they were not being met an automatic adjustment would be made.
3. Develop a program.

4. Establish an operating organization and procedures to support the program in such a manner that the needs identified will be met and such procedures and organizations modifiable on the basis of better serving the purpose.
5. Determine if the needs have been met and if not, make appropriate adjustments in the system.

The college will be responsive to the needs of the community; that is, it will modify its policies, programs, and procedures based on the feedback it receives from the community. The question is: Will it do it in a systematic, preplanned manner, reactively, or will it take the other alternative, which is to compromise the goals and purposes of the institution?

I know of a college that says its basic purpose is to serve the educational needs of youth and adults both in the college district and in the state. Yet within a three-year period, the in-district enrollment of the institution dropped 20 percent while its overall enrollment increased and the total public school population in the district grew. There were indications of this trend each year. The alternative selected here, even if by default, was the latter, to compromise the purpose of the institution until the last year, when action was taken which was *reactive*. Attention to the communication paradigm and utilization of the communication process could have reduced the effect of this problem by making early adjustments.

Those who represent the college must make contacts and establish lines of communication as described in the model in Chapter 5, with educational institutions, industry, organizations, business, and the other segments of the community. But the *establishment* of these lines is merely the first step.

The critical second step is to describe the type of information that will be communicated. The college, to serve its central purpose, must identify educational needs. Therefore, what kind of information is necessary in order for it to make these decisions?

Two general types of information will be received:

1. Identification information, which consists of data about:
   What is, what exists, what people do on a day-to-day basis in the community;
   Discrepancies that exist between what is and what needs to be. What behavior does the "successful" person possess that the unsuccessful one does not?
   What the individual perceives his needs to be.

2. How well are graduates doing in the community? This information is collected from employers, associates, and other persons in the community who interact with the graduate.

Data on the graduates from assessment of their behavioral repertory. What behaviors have they lost (were not reinforced) since they completed the particular course of study? We need to determine what skills, knowledge, and attitudes are utilitarian. We find this out by giving the final (mastery) tests in each course to a selected sampling of master (successful by whatever standard the community wishes to measure success) members of the community. Those behaviors not possessed by a high percentage of these people might well be considered for elimination from the curriculum, and those they do possess, retained. Further analysis of their day-to-day performance might also generate additional requirements.

Data emanating from the graduate's perception of his course of study.

The college must communicate with all aspects of the community in a variety of ways. These lines of communication are shown in the model (Figs. 5-15 through 5-22).

1.0 *consumer*—direct recipient of service within community

2.0 *community*—a collection of persons who are the source of the "needs" to be met by the college

3.0 *educational institutions*—high schools, colleges, universities, vocational schools, technical schools, and other institutions whose primary business is training or education

4.0 *organizations*—unions, craft guilds, professional societies, and other organizations concerned with standards for job or societal performance in any form

5.0 *government*—local, state, and national government executive offices, agencies, and bureaus; legislative and judicial. Regulatory, aid, and legislative lines should be particularly well established

6.0 *supporting information and technology*—sources of data such as ERIC clearing houses, professional societies, research organizations, the U.S. Office of Education, producers of educational materials and products, industry and business or other groups involved in varying kinds of applied or basic research activities, such as private foundations

7.0 *disciplines*—the basic sciences, the physical, social, and humanities; and other areas of human knowledge that traditionally have comprised the content of our curriculums, but will now provide the vehicle by which certain skills and processes are developed in members of the community

Lines of communication must also be established within the college organization. This is shown in Figures 5-16 and 5-17. The policy system, which is comprised of representatives of those served (student body—community), is linked with the management system. The management system communicates with the administrative support system, whose principal function is logistics, and the instructional system, whose principal task is to optimize the learning process.

Communication is the most critical facilitating element in the organization. Without such lines of communication as described above, the college can only be responsive to the needs of the community reactively. Therefore, it will not be able to achieve its purpose: serving the educational needs of youths and adults in the community economically, in terms of resources or trauma.

Communication is not one-way; it is the continuing transmission and reception of messages which are given meaning by the receiver. The college must therefore be sensitive to the receiver and to his transmissions, so that his needs will be correctly identified. Validation must be a fundamental part of the entire communication task. *No* message must be sent without a confirmation of the message having been understood. If the receiver places an interpretation that was not intended by the college, then the message must be modified until it conveys the intended meaning. All of this means that not only must lines of communication be established, but validation criteria must be devised to insure that communication actually takes place.

An important aspect of the transmission and reception of information lies in the content of the message to be communicated. Messages should be coded so they carry appropriate meaning for the receiver, while the receiver must not only be able to decode the symbols, he must apply the same meaning as the sender intended. Remember that this is the responsibility of the originator of the message, not the receiver. A message from the president to a governing board, that a recent breakthrough in brain wave research, as translated to the field of cybernetics, will have a significant effect on the organization of learning environments, is important. This message is perhaps encoded most comprehensively, yet succinctly, with a two-line mathematical formula; yet this would probably not be the most appropriate encoding when the receiver is considered.

The content must stand the test of interpretation by the receiver.

As you look at the arrows in each figure of the model in Chapter 5, it becomes apparent that the information system for a college is going to be complex. We should not be distracted by this complexity, however; these are only the flows. More important than this is the *information* that is transmitted. But *most critical is the processing of this information and resulting system modification. This is the key to effectiveness in institutional communications.* Let's look at an example.

Information is received from a continuing graduate follow-up (described above), stating that graduates employed in certain technical areas are not performing satisfactorily on the job. This deficiency has been traced to an inability to read technical change orders. What happens to this information? Criteria must be established that will guide the processing and any action taken that is based on this data. This particular information enters the college as an input to the management system. It arrives as "the number of persons holding jobs classified as technical, that were fired or changed jobs in the past year."

A criterion has already been established by the college: whenever an employee is fired, certain specified information is to be collected so that the cause can be ascertained. If it is determined to be an educational or training problem, the program can be modified accordingly for future graduates, as well as for the individual who lost the job. A second criterion says that if more than 50 percent changed jobs in a single area, an investigation of the causes would be undertaken. Both of these criteria require no management decision; they provide for automatic adjustment. The data collected on the causes for firing show that 25 percent of the managers list inability to carry out written orders as the reason. They note that the employees are cooperative and willing workers, but they just can't do the job. Some 50 percent of the employees gave the following reason for leaving: "I don't understand the manager's instructions." When tested, only 10 percent of the employees failed to respond to job-oriented oral instructions, while 75 percent failed to respond to similar written instructions.

This data was provided by the management system to the manager or dean of instruction who, after consultation with his appropriate faculty, made the decision to teach the required skills. This and similar decisions made with a certain degree of frequency soon provide enough data on each variable so that criteria can be set for automatic adjustment when the decision falls within certain parameters, thus freeing the dean for more critical instructional decision making.

Let's trace the effect of this decision through the model. There is no change in the basic policy, so adjustment is made by modifying the curriculum within the instructional subsystem. The flow of information proceeds from "receive inputs and analyze" to "formulate program recommendations and decisions" to the "policy and procedures" block to "allocate resources," then to the instructional block where it enters the curriculum and guidance subsystems at (.1) and proceeds through each to instruction (.4), where students being prepared for technical fields are given more appropriate decoding skills.

This continuing modification based on feedback is an ongoing process in the college. Many adjustments, to begin with, have to be made by management decision, but as data is collected, more and more of the adjustments can be made automatically. When the proficiency of the graduates drops below a certain level, this adjustment is made; or when a need of a certain priority is discovered, the system goes to work to meet the need. As the system becomes more sophisticated and effective, the need for competent, well-educated human beings becomes more and more apparent. Initial decisions made on little information will be modified until a good decision emerges by successive approximation.

We have only scratched the surface in determining what the communications requirements for a college are in order to make it adaptive. Yet without this adaptive capability the college cannot acccomplish its purpose of serving the educational needs of community members. To summarize: the lines of communication must be established, information requirements specified, and criteria developed for processing information system adjustment based on the data. If, due to insufficient data or other reason, criteria cannot be established at this time, a management decision must be made in each case until sufficient information does exist on which to base criteria. The intended goal is that no management decisions be made at the sub-policy level. Ideally, this means that a policy, once translated into an operation, should be carried out through automatic adjustment of the system. The role of the manager is to keep the information lines open, set criteria for decision making, and develop new policy recommendations. The manager, as a matter of routine, should not make day-to-day operational decisions; these should be performed by automatic adjustment based on established criteria.

Objectives based on the purpose of the institution are constantly being generated, modified, and discarded, based on the real requirements. All programs, elements, and aspects of the college are adaptive and sensitive to the needs of the community, which now become more than empty words.

You may wonder how in the world you get faculty and staff for such a dynamic institution requiring different skills than have ever been exercised and different roles than have ever been the custom in the more traditional college. Let's look at the requirements for such an institution:

All activities—instructional, management, and administrative support—should be managed by objective. These objectives should at all times reflect the goals of the school and support the learning system—the student interacting with the learning environment.

No objective, once established, should be cast in concrete, but all should remain open to modification based on empirical evidence.

Management objectives must not dictate instructional objectives and procedures, but the reverse should be true.

The system, including the faculty with their support personnel, should be accountable for student learning. The policy-making group must be educated to their role in optimizing student learning. Most board members perceive their role as policy making, but how they arrive at policy and determine when it is or is not accomplishing the goal is another matter.

When a board establishes an instructional program for the persons they serve, they must set a standard or level of evidence that will permit them to say with confidence, "We have a good instructional program. Our students are learning and we are moving toward our goals."

Objectives must be established at all levels to serve as a basis for improving the program. If students cannot perform a compression test on an automobile to certain specifications as described in the objective, the program must be modified. Students who cannot compression-test the car will have to stay with that objective until they meet it.

The tasks that must be performed in each system within the college require skills and roles that do not exist in most institutions.

The role of an instructor in the model is to manage the learning of students. He calls on curriculum and instructional designers and producers to develop the materials and processes needed to bring about learning. He depends on other specialists to assess student learning characteristics and determine the needs and other functions described in the model. The instructor is responsible for student learning to a dean or manager of instruction who, in turn, is responsible to the president. The president is responsible to the community (the student body) for meeting their educational needs.

A problem encountered by nearly every institution attempting to improve instruction by following an audio-tutorial or systems methodology (you'll note that I am not necessarily talking about one using a systems approach) has been the expectation that faculty perform all of the functions. They were supposed to develop curriculum, construct materials, validate them, diagnose, prescribe, test, assess student learning characteristics, and still be civil to their spouses and children—that is, if they were ever home. This is humanly impossible if the tasks are listed, described, and timed. Something has to "give," and normally does. The instructor is usually reduced to covering material as he did before.

An analogous situation is the role of the medical doctor. The instructor, like the doctor, does not have to develop, test, or mix his own drugs, except in unusual circumstances. *He does, on the other hand, diagnose, prescribe, and observe the effects.* He modifies subsequent prescriptions based on the effects.

Let's look in on an instructor who is attempting to take a systems approach to his instructional program and is doing a creditable job in a traditional institution. Assume that you are the president of this institution. In Communications 104 the instructor has as the objective of his lecture today the following:

> The student will complete an exercise such as the one shown below, without error. The specific words may be slightly altered, but the basic content must remain the same.

The acceptable responses to the exercise are:

Topic Sentence: The strong religion of the Hebrews affected a wide range of activity in the Hebrew civilization.
    A. theocratic political organization developed
    B. social activity regulated
    C. art reflected religious law
    D. literature reveals religious beliefs
Conclusion: Influence wide and strong

OBJECTIVE: You will complete an exercise like the one below without any mistakes after you have completed the instruction. This exercise is to determine how well you can do now.

DIRECTION: Outline the paragraph below in the space provided.

Topic Sentence: ....

    A. ....

    B. ....

    C. ....

    D. ....

Conclusion ....

Make each statement A-D and the conclusion as explicit and concise as possible. Each point A-D is to be consistent with the topic sentence and lead to the conclusion.

SAMPLE PARAGRAPH:

The Influence of Religion on Hebrew Civilization

The strong religion of the Hebrews affected a wide range of activity in the Hebrew civilization. The leaders who assumed their power to rule because God chose them developed a theocratic form of government. Social activity such as the educational program spoken of many times in the books of Moses, was controlled by the tribe of Levi, appointed by God to take care of priestly tasks. Also in accordance with God's will, the artistic efforts of the Hebrews were directed toward adornment which did not violate the commandment against graven images. The complications of religious writing of the Hebrews further reveal the complete dedication of scribes, priests, and teachers whose task it was to record the religious and tribal laws, the history, and the poetic praise of the Lord God of the Hebrews. The range of influence exerted by religion was wide and the power exerted was strong.

Figure 7-1. Sample of the Test Given to Determine
Whether a Student Meets the Objective.

There are 200 students enrolled in Communications 104 and the instructor normally meets the class in four sections, with 50 students in each section. The routine in each class is to review the preceding day's material and then go on to the new material. But beginning today, the instructor is going to innovate. The first innovation is to describe the objective to the students in terms of the test as shown in Figure 7-1. Then instead of meeting four sections, he meets all 200 students and gives them the pretest. He finds that 30 students already meet the objective before he does anything. Because he hasn't planned anything else for them to do, he gives them the option of going to the library or sitting in on his lecture. Most elect to go to the library. As long as he has the 170 students together, he lectures to all of them at one time. He concludes with the post-test, which is the same as the pretest, except that it uses different content. To his dismay he finds that only five students meet the objective. At the next class meeting he reviews the same material with his groups of 50. Ten more students meet the objective, leaving 155 students who have not. So he works up some practice exercises, not only for the ones who haven't made it, but also for those who have, so they may go on to the next several objectives which he has worked out. After a month of this, our innovative friend is nearly out of his mind. Some of his students are on Objective #150 and others are still—no, not still struggling with #104—but are back on #35, with a few on Objectives #1, #5, and #6. The instructor's problem is not new. It has been with him for some time, ever since he had any students. But now he is *recognizing it.* Students are different; they learn in different ways, at different rates and perhaps, most importantly, they learn (modify their behavior) strictly in terms of what they perceive the consequences of this learning to be.

Sadly, this instructor may soon give up because, having taken a "systems approach," he has identified problems he did not perceive before; and the constraints he identifies make it impossible, based on his findings, to get more than 50 percent of the students to perform at an acceptable level in Communications 104. He comes to you, the president, with this evidence and spreads the following information across your desk:

His objectives stated behaviorally and the criterion tests he uses to measure attainment of them.

The constraints delimited

time

material resources

personnel

schedule

He has laid out several alternate solutions which require substantial support in all of the areas noted above, to modify the constraints. He needs your help here to identify other alternatives and manipulate constraints so they become variables where possible. (What is a constraint to him may well be a variable to you, and likewise what may be a constraint to you may be a variable to your governing board.)

In working through what this instructor has done in the manner described in these guidelines, one thing becomes apparent: to have all of the students presently enrolled in Communications 104 meet the objectives that have been set is going to cost more than could be provided in the budget. You ask yourself, why not go to the governing board and have them make a decision on the objectives? So you work up three alternatives, each involving a reduction in the number of objectives to be met; that is, either certain students are eliminated or certain objectives are modified or eliminated. At the next board meeting you and your instructor make the presentation. The board, struck by the possibilities of the idea, ask you to work up similar alternatives for every course and program in the college. You soon find yourself in a position similar to that of the instructor at the end of the first month of innovation—aware of the problems but at a loss about how to solve them.

The "systems approach" is the obvious tool to use. In order for you to work up even a college-wide feasibility study, it is necessary to employ the process. The instructor in 104 will stop wasting time lecturing and direct the development of certain materials and describe certain activities his students may perform. Just how effective our innovative friend becomes depends on the support we give him.

Our instructor is not a typical college faculty member. In fact, one of the most critical problems of an institution lies in the selection and retention of flexible, competent, and dedicated personnel to make the system work. Below are some ideas along these lines which, based on the study, appear to be important:

1. Make a full and complete commitment to solving problems by this approach at all levels. This means a commitment from all personnel.
2. Secure from the outset, communications and information expertise to develop a *comprehensive* communication and information system for the college to meet the requirements established by the model.

3. Employ *dedicated and flexible* faculty members for *instruction* whose primary reinforcement is not derived from presentational activities but from seeing students become increasingly competent learners. Be willing to commit substantial resources to training and reinforcement on an institution-wide basis. *Don't expect instructors to perform as curriculum materials developers* unless you train them *extensively* and release them from instructional responsibilities.

4. Provide competent support teams in *curriculum and guidance,* once more making a heavy commitment to training.

5. The administrative support system must tailor its organization, procedures, and total operation to the support of instruction. This system exists *only* to facilitate learning. Therefore competent personnel in each support area, committed to the purposes and philosophies of the institution, should be secured.

6. Likewise, the management system exists to facilitate achieving the purpose of the college. The manager or dean of instruction becomes the key individual in this process, with the communication and information specialists playing a critical role and a number of management specialists making up the team.

7. The president oversees the entire operation, must be the sole liaison with the policy system, and must be responsible for the proper translation of policy to programs.

8. A job description should be developed for each position, based on the organization that emerges from these functions. It is wise to start with a clean organizational chart and no preconceived notions about what it should look like. Let it develop strictly on the basis of function, allowing "form to follow function," as in architecture.

9. It should be noted that because of the adaptive nature of the institution, positions will be created, eliminated, and modified on a continuing basis as educational needs change, creating continual demands for retraining.

10. In the training of personnel to operate the college, the same theory of instruction holds and the same procedures and processes should be employed as with students. Begin with each individual's perception of reality and then help him to modify that perception to more closely conform to reality. For example, an instructor who says that his principal problem in instruction is "time to cover more material" sees this as the major stumbling block to his effectiveness. The reality of the situation, however, is that the student is not learning what he, the instructor, and the college have agreed he should learn and that the real reason is that the student does

not have the prerequisites for such learning. The instructor who is given more "time to cover more material" finds that the student is still not learning. Under these circumstances it is likely that the instructor's perception of the real problem would change. Your task is to see to it that this happens with each member of your faculty and staff. A focus on student learning is equally important for your business manager, director of student personnel services, and buildings and grounds director.

SUMMARY

Decisions made without information and an underlying process providing feedback on the effects of those decisions are not only ineffective but dangerous. A decision based on the information available may be modified when its effects are known. A communications system should be developed that provides relevant information to be used in decision making.

The college must be committed to employing a systems approach that uses this information in the decision-making process and the information on effects of the decision, to modify subsequent decisions.

Since each institution is a unique system made up of interrelated components, they should all be pulling together toward realization of the goals of the college. There is no one right series of steps to follow, but there is a process. By seriously exercising this process, mankind has performed some fantastic feats, including landing men on the moon. It is paradoxical, as Lieberman has suggested, to think that this same process is not currently being applied to man's most important enterprise—education.

As with any powerful tool, there is danger involved in its use. Education may become effective—a student's behavior may truly be modified in predetermined ways. Someday educators may come to the position of the scientist who creates the ultimate device that may be used for the selective annihilation of mankind or for his total preservation and fulfillment. Who should make the decision on which it is to be? The scientist has already encountered this problem. Someday the social scientist and the educational engineer may face a similar problem, as an applied science of education emerges.

The field of education today is in a prescientific state with vastly more applicable knowledge and technology available than is being applied. The endless criticism of education is useless unless it is accompanied by alternatives to what exists. Hopefully this study will be perceived by community college educators, those in institutions at the community level, as providing a start toward viable alternatives.

The existing knowledge and technology, if applied, could begin a movement toward the development of an educational institution capable of identifying and meeting the educational needs of each community member—its goal being education for a dynamic society founded on democratic ideals. In such an institution the individual would be at the center of the system; he would be prepared for increasing humanity in a dynamic environment requiring continual modification of his behavior. Such an institution would not impose the standards of the present society on future generations, but would provide the individual with educational skills for establishing standards on a continuing basis, suitable to the ever-changing society. It would recognize each individual as an idiosyncratic learner who modifies his behavior based on his perception of the consequences. The college would prepare and equip the individual for true freedom and develop within each person the inborn capacity to love.

It is proposed that the institution utilize existing knowledge through the process of technology—the systems approach—to achieve these ideals.

The community college—as the most recent sibling of our educational system, born of the twentieth century, uncluttered by tradition, committed to the instruction of its cast-offs, strengthened by local commitment and moving toward accountability to the learner—is the logical place for education to begin to face its challenge and prove its commitment and indispensable worth to society.

Notes

Chapter 1

1. Edmund J. Gleazer, Jr., "The Community College, What Is It—A New Social Invention?", undated brochure of the American Association of Junior Colleges, Washington, D.C., 1965[?].
2. John L. Burns, "Our Era of Opportunity," *Saturday Review,* January 14, 1967, p. 39.
3. University of Southern California Occasional Report #9, Los Angeles, 1967, p. 5.
4. B. Lamar Johnson, *Islands of Innovation Expanding: Changes in the Community College,* Beverly Hills, Calif.: Glencoe Press, 1969, pp. 91-114.
5. John Tirrell, "Program Innovation," paper presented to the Council of North Central Junior Colleges, Denver, Colorado, October 3, 1966, p. 3.
6. *Ibid.*
7. *Ibid.,* p. 112.
8. David E. Barbee and L. William Motzel, "Core Objective #1—A Systems Approach to the Design of Instructional Systems," Washington, D.C.: The Catholic University, 1968, unpublished paper.

Chapter 2

1. Myron Lieberman, "Big Business, Technology and Education," *Phi Delta Kappan,* January 1967, p. 25.
2. Hilda Taba, *Curriculum Development: Theory and Practice,* New York: Harcourt, Brace and World, 1962, p. 54.
3. Jerome S. Bruner, *Toward a Theory of Instruction,* Cambridge, Mass.: The Belknap Press of Harvard University Press, 1966, p. 25.
4. John Kenneth Galbraith, *The New Industrial State,* Boston: Houghton Mifflin, 1967, pp. 12-13.

5. By permission. From *Webster's Third New International Dictionary,* © 1966 by G&C Merriam Co., Publishers of the Merriam-Webster Dictionaries.

6. Bruner, *Theory of Instruction,* p. 1.

7. *Ibid.,* p. 113.

8. *Ibid.,* p. 171.

9. Ivor K. Davies, "The Mathetics Style of Programming," *Programmed Learning and the Language Laboratory,* Collected papers, Klaus Bung, editor, London: Longmac, 1967, p. 31.

10. Ivor K. Davies, Introduction to "Review of Educational Cybernetics and Applied Linguistics," in *Recall,* Supplement 1, March 1969, pp. 9-10.

11. Francis Mechner and Donald A. Cook, "Behavior Technology and Manpower Development," background paper prepared for the Organization for Economic Cooperation and Development by Basic Systems, New York, 1964, pp. 1-2.

12. E. L. Thorndike, *Animal Intelligence: Experimental Studies,* New York: Macmillan, 1911.

13. B. F. Skinner, *The Behavior of Organisms: An Experimental Analysis,* New York: Appleton-Century-Crofts, 1938.

14. Rice Berkeley, article in *New York Times Magazine,* March 17, 1968, © 1968 by The New York Times Company. Reprinted by permission.

15. B. F. Skinner, *Walden Two,* New York: Macmillan, 1948.

16. Mechner and Cook, "Behavior Technology," p. 2.

17. *Ibid.,* pp. 3-4.

18. Lloyd E. Homme, "Behavioral Engineering in Instructional Systems," paper presented at the Minuteman Instructional Systems Planning Conference, Autonetics, Anaheim, California, November 6, 1964.

19. *Ibid.,* p. 23.

20. *Ibid.,* p. 24.

21. Harold L. Cohen, "Educational Therapy: The Design of Learning Environments," and "Appendix A," *Research in Psychotherapy,* vol. 3, 1968, Washington, D.C.: The American Psychological Association, Inc., pp. 21-53.

22. Lloyd E. Homme, "A Behavior Technology Exists—Here and Now," in *Technology and Innovation in Education,* Aerospace Education Foundation, New York: Praeger, 1968.

23. J. W. Atkinson and P. O'Connor, "Effects of Ability Grouping in Schools Related to Individual Differences in Achievement-Related Motivation," a U.S. Office of Education, Cooperative Research Program, Project 1283, University of Michigan, 1963.

24. Edwin A. Locke, "Motivational Effects of Knowledge of Results," American Institute for Research, Washington Office, 1967.

25. Thomas F. Gilbert, "Praxeonomy: A Systematic Approach to Identifying Training Needs," in *Management of Personnel Quarterly,* Bureau of Industrial Relations, University of Michigan, vol. 6, no. 3, pp. 20-33.

26. U.S. Forest Service Manual, *A Guide to Analyzing Instructional Needs,* Washington, D.C.: Department of Agriculture, TT-7-[6140], pp. 2-6.

27. *Ibid.,* pp. 2-11 through 2-26.

28. Davies, Introduction, p. 15.

29. Thomas F. Gilbert, "Mathetics: The Technology of Education," *Journal of Mathetics,* University of Alabama, 1962, as reprinted in *Recall,* Supplement 1, March 1969, p. 23.

30. *Ibid.,* p. 22.

31. *Ibid.*

32. *Ibid.,* p. 23.

33. James L. Evans, "Programming in Mathematics and Logic," in R. Glaser, ed., *Teaching Machines and Programmed Learning,* Washington, D.C.: National Education Association, Department of Audiovisual Instruction, 1965.

34. Gilbert, "Mathetics," pp. 47-50.

35. James L. Evans, "The Technology of Doing Your Own Thing—A Nonpaper on the Nonfuture of Noneducation," prepared for the Seventh Annual Convention of the National Society for Programmed Instruction, Washington, D.C., April 1969.

36. Paul Saettler, "Instructional Technology: Some Concerns and Desiderata," *AV Communication Review,* vol. 17, no. 4, Winter 1969, DAVI-NEA, Washington, D.C., p. 359.

37. Norbert Wiener, *Cybernetics; or Control and Communication in the Animal and the Machine,* Cambridge, Mass.: MIT Press, 1961.

38. Karl U. Smith and Margaret Foltz Smith, *Cybernetic Principles of Learning and Educational Design,* New York: Holt, Rinehart & Winston, 1966, p. 471.

39. *Ibid.,* p. 211.

40. *Ibid.,* p. 475.

41. *Ibid.,* p. 477.

42. *Ibid.*

43. *Ibid.*

44. *Ibid.,* p. 476.

45. *Ibid.,* p. 382.

46. *Ibid.,* pp. 475-476.

47. *Ibid.,* p. 478.

48. *Ibid.,* pp. 477-478.

49. Charles F. Jones, "Steersman, Mind Thine Oar!" *The Humble Way,* vol. 8, no. 4, Fourth Quarter, 1969, p. 1.

Chapter 3

1. Taba, *Curriculum Development,* p. 8.

2. *Ibid.,* p. 10.

3. *Ibid.*

4. John Franklin Bobbitt, *The Curriculum,* Boston: Houghton Mifflin, 1918, p. 76.

5. Emmie and Henry M. Felkin, *The Science of Education,* Boston: D. C. Heath & Co., 1893.

6. Charles H. Judd, "The Scientific Technique of Curriculum Making," *School & Society,* vol. 15, no. 367, January 1922.

7. Bobbitt, *The Curriculum,* p. 76.

8. *Ibid.,* p. 76.

9. John Franklin Bobbitt, *Curriculum Making in Los Angeles,* Chicago: University of Chicago Press, 1922, p. 6.

10. *Ibid.*

11. Harold Rugg, ed., *Curriculum Making: Past and Present,* Twenty-sixth Yearbook, National Society for the Study of Education, Chicago: University of Chicago Press, 1926, p. 54.

12. *Ibid.,* pp. 38-39.

13. *Ibid.*

14. Bobbitt, *Curriculum Making.*

15. Elliot W. Eisner, "Educational Objectives: Help or Hindrance?" *School Review* 75:250-60, 277-82.

16. Boyd H. Bode, *Modern Educational Theories*, New York: Macmillan, 1927, p. 110.

17. *Ibid.*, p. 112.

18. David Snedden, *Sociological Determination of Objectives in Education*, Philadelphia: J. B. Lippincott, 1921, p. 15.

19. David Snedden, *Problems of Educational Readjustment*, Boston: Houghton Mifflin, 1913, p. 71.

20. W. W. Charters, *Curriculum Construction*, New York: Macmillan, 1923.

21. Charles McMurry, *How to Organize the Curriculum*, New York: Macmillan, 1923.

22. W. H. Kilpatrick, *The Project Method*, pamphlet, Teachers College, N.Y.: Columbia University Press, 1919.

23. J. A. Stevenson, *The Project Method of Teaching*, New York: Macmillan, 1921.

24. E. Collins, *An Experiment with a Project Curriculum*, New York: Macmillan, 1923.

25. Bode, *Modern Educational Theories*, p. 147.

26. *Ibid.*, p. 148.

27. *Ibid.*, pp. 149-151.

28. McMurry, *How to Organize the Curriculum.*

29. Bode, *Modern Educational Theories*, p. 165.

30. John Dewey, *Experience and Education*, New York: Collier Books, 1938, p. 10; material used by permission of Kappa Delta Pi, An Honor Society in Education, owners of the copyright.

31. Goodlad, John I., "Curriculum: State of the Field," *Review of Educational Research*, vol. 39, no. 3, June 1969, p. 285.

32. *Ibid.*

33. *Ibid.*, p. 374.

34. *Ibid.*, p. 368.

35. All research findings are drawn from the American Educational Research Association, *Review of Educational Research*, vol. 39, no. 3, June 1969.

36. *Ibid.*, p. 309.

37. *Ibid.*, p. 303.

38. *Ibid.*, p. 371.

39. *Ibid.*, p. 372.

40. *Ibid.*, p. 319.

41. *Ibid.*, p. 319.

42. *Ibid.*, p. 335.

43. *Ibid.*, p. 354.

44. *Ibid.*

45. *Ibid.*, p. 359.

46. *Ibid.*, p. 371.

47. *Ibid.*, p. 372.

48. *Ibid.*, p. 343.

49. *Ibid.*

50. *Ibid.*, p. 312.

51. *Ibid.*

52. *Ibid.*, p. 369.

53. Taba, *Curriculum Development*, p. 7.

54. Jerome S. Bruner, *Toward a Theory of Instruction*, Cambridge, Mass.: The Belknap Press of Harvard University Press, 1966, p. 32.

55. *Ibid.*, p. 33.

56. *Ibid.*
57. Smith and Smith, *Cybernetic Principles,* p. 478.
58. Taba, *Curriculum Development,* p. 42.
59. *Ibid.*
60. *Ibid.,* pp. 41-42.
61. *Ibid.*
62. Bruner, *Theory of Instruction,* p. 126.
63. Taba, *Curriculum Development,* p. 47.
64. *Ibid.,* p. 75.
65. Norbert Wiener, *The Human Use of Human Beings,* New York: Doubleday, A Doubleday Anchor Book, 1954, p. 114.
66. *Ibid.,* p. 116.
67. *Ibid.,* p. 129.
68. *Ibid.,* p. 130.
69. *Ibid.,* p. 128.
70. *Ibid.,* p. 73.
71. *Ibid.,* p. 278.

Chapter 4

1. Dewey, *Experience and Education,* p. 28.
2. Bode, *Modern Educational Theories,* p. 238.
3. Bruner, *Toward a Theory of Instruction,* p. 22.
4. *Ibid.,* p. 25.

Chapter 5

1. Banathy, *Instructional Systems,* p. 16.
2. Leonard C. Silvern, *Systems Engineering of Education; I: The Evolution of Systems Thinking in Education,* Los Angeles: Education and Training Consultants Co., 1971, p. 1.
3. Francis Mechner and Donald Cook, "Behavior Technology and Manpower Development," a background paper prepared for the Organization for Economic Cooperation and Development by Basic Systems, New York, N.Y., 1964, pp. 14-16.
4. C. R. Carpenter, "Approaches to Promising Areas of Research in the Field of Instructional Television," *New Teaching Aids for the American Classroom,* Stanford, Cal.: The Institute for Communications Research, Stanford University, 1960, pp. 75-76.
5. United States National Commission on Technology, Automation, and Economic Progress, Report, February 1966, Washington, D.C., p. 99.
6. Barbee and Motzel, *Core Objective #1,* pp. 2-3.
7. Banathy, *Instructional Systems,* p. 13.
8. Silvern, *Systems Engineering,* p. 1.
9. *Ibid.,* p. 5.
10. *Ibid.,* pp. 1-15.
11. *Ibid.,* p. 10.
12. W. W. Charters, "The Era of the Educational Engineer," *Educational Research Bulletin,* December 1951, pp. 233-234.
13. Silvern, *Systems Engineering,* pp. 8-11.
14. Charters, "Era of the Educational Engineer," p. 237.

15. At this writing a National Educational Technology bill is pending in the Congress.

16. Gabriel D. Ofiesh, "Tomorrow's Educational Engineers," *Educational Technology*, July 15, 1968, p. 5.

17. Charters, "Era of the Educational Engineer," p. 237.

18. D. Wolfle, "Training," *Handbook of Experimental Psychology*, S. S. Stevens, ed., New York: John Wiley, 1951, p. 1,280.

19. L. C. Silvern, "Guide to the State Fire Training Program," State Division of Safety, Albany, N.Y., 1951.

20. Silvern, *Systems Engineering*, pp. 38-39.

21. Wolfle, "Training," p. 1,280.

22. Silvern, p. 42.

23. *Ibid.*, p. 16.

24. *Ibid.*, p. 46.

25. *Ibid.*, p. 60.

26. J. W. and M. W. Riley, "Sociological Perspectives on the Use of New Educational Media," *New Teaching Aids for the American Classroom: A Symposium on the State of Research in Instructional Television and Tutorial Machines*, Stanford, Cal.: Stanford University Press, 1959, 1960, p. 27.

27. G. Pask, "Adaptive Teaching with Adaptive Machines," in *Teaching Machines and Programmed Learning*, Lumsdaine and Glaser, eds., Washington, D.C.: National Education Association, Department of Audiovisual Instruction, 1960, p. 362.

28. Silvern, *Systems Engineering*, p. 62.

29. J. W. Forrester, "Systems Technology and Industrial Dynamics," *MIT Technology Review*, June 1957.

30. Robert Heinich, "A System of Instructional Management," unpublished paper, November 1962, later amplified in *Technology and the Management of Instruction*, Association for Educational Communications and Technology, 1970.

31. B. Morris, "The Function of Media in the Public Schools," *Audiovisual Instruction*, January 1963, p. 12.

32. Systems Analysis Committee Proposal, p. 1, unpublished paper.

33. Gabriel D. Ofiesh, "Results of an Air Force Study of Programmed Instruction," remarks at a symposium of Division 19 (military psychology), American Psychological Association Annual Conference, 4 September 1963, p. 93.

34. *Ibid.*

35. Center for Instructional Communications, Syracuse University, unpublished, undated paper.

36. Robert G. Smith, Jr., *The Design of Instructional Systems*, Technical Report 66-18 of the Human Resources Research Office (HumRRO), November 1966, Washington, D.C.: George Washington University.

37. Leonard C. Silvern, "Introduction," *Educational Technology*, vol. 9, no. 6, June 1969, p. 3.

38. T. Antoinette Ryan, "Systems Techniques for Programs of Counseling and Counselor Education," *Educational Technology*, vol. 9, no. 6, June 1969, pp. 9-10.

39. S. N. Postlethwait, J. Novak, and H. Murray, *An Integrated Experience Approach to Learning*, Minneapolis: Burgess Publishing Co., 1964.

40. S. N. Postlethwait, "Instructional Techniques," abstract, n.d., Purdue University, unpublished paper, p. 3.

41. *Ibid.*, pp. 3-5.

42. Postlethwait *et al.*, *Integrated Experience*, p. 19.

43. *Ibid.*, pp. 19-21.

44. *Ibid.,* pp. 82-85.

45. John Tirrell, "Some Reflections on 150 Man-Years Using the Systems Approach in an Open-Door College," occasional paper, B. Lamar Johnson, ed., University of California at Los Angeles, 1967, pp. 57-58.

46. Tirrell, "Program Innovation," pp. 4, 7, 11.

47. The Continuation Education System Development Project, Leon East, project director, La Puente, Cal., unpublished, undated, brief description.

48. Mary Ann Hammerel and W. J. Laidlaw, report prepared for the study of Instructional Technology, Academy for Educational Development, Inc.

49. *Ibid.,* pp. 12-13.

50. *Ibid.,* p. 13.

51. *Ibid.,* p. 14.

52. *Ibid.,* pp. 14-15.

53. *Ibid.,* pp. 15-16.

54. *Ibid.,* p. 17.

55. *Ibid.,* p. 21.

56. *Ibid.,* p. 22.

57. *Ibid.,* p. 23.

58. *Ibid.*

59. *Colorado Mountain College:* "Colorado Mountain College; An Adventure in Modern Learning," unpublished paper, 1966, pp. 9-10.

60. Arthur M. Suchesk, "Southern California Regional Occupational Center: A New Environment for Industrial Education," report to the Second Annual National Laboratory for the Advancement of Education, Washington, D.C., January 1970, p. 2.

61. *Ibid.,* p. 4.

62. *Ibid.,* pp. 4-5.

63. *Ibid.,* pp. 5-6.

64. For specific guidance, see U.S. Forest Service Manual, *A Guide to Analyzing Instructional Needs,* Washington, D.C.: Department of Agriculture, 11-7-(6140).

Chapter 6

1. Interview with Richard Wilson, January 1970. Wilson is the director of the New Institutions project of the American Association of Junior Colleges.

2. Benjamin S. Bloom and D. R. Krathwohl, *Taxonomy of Educational Objectives; I: Cognitive Domain,* New York: David McKay, 1967.

Chapter 7

1. U.S. Forest Service, Manual, *Guide to Analyzing Instructional Needs.*

Glossary

adjustment (of the system)   A process whereby the system is modified so that its product more nearly meets predetermined standards and/or to make the system more efficient and economical.

analysis   The breaking down of information or material into its constituent parts for the purpose of determining relationships that may exist between the parts or the way they are organized.

components   Parts which comprise a system and which are selected to service specific functions required for the attainment of the objectives of the system.

constraints   Known limitations and restrictions in the environmental conditions and the capabilities of human and material resources involved in the design, development, and maintenance of a system.

criterion test   An instrument used to assess the degree to which a student meets predetermined performance objectives.

curriculum   A body of prescribed learning experiences which are derived on the basis of stated aims translated to specific objectives. The outcome, student learning, is used to validate the learning experiences and evaluate the objectives.

education   The process of acquiring the behaviors necessary to learn; in other words, learning how to learn.

evaluation   The process of determining the appropriateness of the system objectives when tested in the "real world." This is accomplished by sending students who have met the objectives of the system out into the society to determine empirically, by their success or failure, the validity of the objectives. For example, a system may turn out fine Stanley Steamer mechanics but in the society there is no demand for such mechanics. The system may be said to be valid, but inappropriate, when evaluated.

feedback The information derived from a comparison of the output with the anticipated (prescribed) output used for purposes of quality control and system modification.

functions Areas of responsibility that must be serviced in designing, developing, and maintaining a system in order to facilitate the attainment of the objectives of the system.

*__functions analysis__ The process by which the designer of a system identifies whatever is required to be done in order to insure the attainment of objectives. (Bela Banathy, *Instructional Systems* [Palo Alto: Fearon Press, 1968]. Term definitions from this text are identified by asterisk.)

input The raw material that enters the system, to be modified and released as output.

instruction The process of providing the learning environments and management necessary to cause a learner to meet his prespecified objectives.

instructional system A system whose fundamental input is students, that is evaluated on the basis of student learning and exists for no other reason. It has measurably stated objectives, criterion-referenced measurement devices, validated learning strategies which are replicable, and its fundamental output (student learning) is measured and compared with the stated objectives; if a difference exists, the information is fed back to the designer and the system is modified successively until it reaches an acceptable standard. The process is iterative in that the system moves closer and closer to its specified goals by successive approximations.

iterative process To move toward a goal by successive approximation; that is, each trial and modification moves closer and closer to the goal.

learner-centered The learner is at the functional center of the system. The system objectives are stated in terms of learner behavior and all components of the system exist to facilitate that learning.

learning A modification of behavior as measured by a change in response in the individual.

model An abstraction of the real world in order to represent reality. This abstraction consists of a graphic and narrative description which may then be used to "exercise" on paper its components and their interrelationships for modification and adjustment, to insure optimal configuration.

objective A statement that describes in observable and measurable terms the expected output performance of the product of the system.

*__output__ The product of a system; the result or outcome of the processes employed by the system.

*__quality control__ The monitoring of a system and its planned change by which adjustments are introduced to correct for differences between actual output performance and performance expectations established by objectives.

*__subsystem__ A part of a system that is comprised of two or more components. The subsystem has a purpose of its own and is designed to interact with its peer subsystems in order to attain the overall purpose of the system. (As an example, the instructional subsystem and the counseling and administrative subsystems interact by design, making up the system called the school.)

suprasystem   A larger entity designed for a specific purpose, which is comprised of two or more systems.

synthesis   The building up of a new whole by combining the parts in new relationships. It generally occurs in combination with analysis, which is prerequisite.

system   An aggregation or assemblage of elements which are interrelated and interdependent in accomplishing some goal.

technology   The systematic application of scientific or other organized knowledge to the solution of practical problems. (Galbraith)

trade-off   Refers to the cost versus effectiveness studies, the purpose of which is to establish which of the proposed solutions (or what combination of proposed solutions) represent the most effective way of accomplishing the objective at the least cost.

training   The process of acquiring specific skills, knowledges, and attitudes which will prepare an individual for a particular task, whether it be a job or some other task.

validation   The process of successively improving an educational, instructional, or learning system to a predetermined standard by using lack of student progress toward an achievement of measurable objectives as data for system modification. Such a system is termed to be valid when qualified students meet the objectives (to predetermined standards) after proceeding through the learning experiences.

Bibliography

BOOKS

Aerospace Education Foundation. *Technology and Innovation in Education.* Prepared by Aerospace Education Foundation. New York: Praeger Publishers, 1968.

Banathy, Bela. *Instructional Systems.* Belmont, Cal.: Fearon Publishers, 1968.

Berrin, Kenneth F. *General and Social Systems.* New Brunswick, N.J.: Rutgers University Press, 1968.

Bertalanffy, Ludwig von (ed.). *General Systems Yearbook of the Society for the Advancement of General Systems Theory.* Vol. 1, 1956.

Bloom, Benjamin S. *Stability and Change in Human Characteristics.* New York: John Wiley, 1964.

————. and Krathwohl, D.R. *Taxonomy of Educational Objectives; I: Cognitive Domain.* New York: David McKay, 1967.

Bobbitt, John Franklin. *The Curriculum.* Boston: Houghton Mifflin, 1918.

————. *Curriculum Making in Los Angeles.* Chicago: University of Chicago Press, 1922.

————. *The Curriculum of Modern Education.* New York: McGraw-Hill, 1941.

————. . . . *Education 362 (the Curriculum).* Chicago: University of Chicago Press, 1934.

————. *How to Make a Curriculum.* New York: Houghton Mifflin, 1924.

Bobbitt, John Franklin, *et al. Curriculum Investigations.* Chicago: University of Chicago Press, 1926.

Bode, Boyd H. *Modern Educational Theories.* New York: Macmillan, 1927.

Bruner, Jerome S. *Toward a Theory of Instruction.* Cambridge, Mass.: The Belknap Press of Harvard University Press, 1966.

Buckley, Walter (*ed.*). *Modern Systems Research for the Behavioral Scientist.* Chicago, Aldine, 1968.

Caldwell, Lynton K. (*ed.*). *Science, Technology and Public Policy: A Bibliography I.* Bloomington: Department of Government, Indiana University, 1968.

Callahan, Raymond E. *Education and the Cult of Efficiency.* Chicago: University of Chicago Press, 1962.

Carter, Launor F., and Silberman, Harry. *The Systems Approach, Technology and the School.* U. S. Department of Commerce, Institute for Applied Technology, 1965.

Charters, W. W. *Curriculum Construction.* New York: Macmillan, 1923.
————. *Teaching of Ideals.* New York: The Macmillan Co., 1927.

Chestnut, Harold. *Systems Engineering Methods.* New York: Wiley, 1967.
————. *Systems Engineering Tools.* New York: Wiley,1965.

Churchman, C. W., *et al. Introduction to Operations Research.* New York: John Wiley & Sons, 1957.

Collings, Elsworth. *An Experiment with a Project Curriculum,* Chaps. 1-3. New York: The Macmillan Company, 1923.

Coombs, Philip H. *The World Educational Crisis: A Systems Analysis.* New York: Oxford University Press, 1968.

Crary, R. W. *Humanizing the School.* New York: Alfred A. Knopf, 1969.

Cross, Kathryn Patricia. *The Junior College Student.* Princeton: Educational Testing Service, 1968.

Dale, Edgar. *Programmed Instruction.* Chicago: University of Chicago Press, 1967.

Dewey, John. *Experience and Education.* New York: Collier Books, 1938.
————. *The Sources of a Science of Education.* New York: Liveright Publishing, 1929.

Eckman, Donald P. (*ed.*). *Systems: Research and Design.* New York: John Wiley & Sons, 1961.

Edwards, Newton, and Richey, Herman. *The School in the American Social Order.* 2nd ed. Boston: Houghton Mifflin Co., 1963.

Esbensen, Thorwald. *Working with Individualized Instruction: The Duluth Experience.* Palo Alto: Fearon Publishers, 1968.

Eurich, Alvin C. (ed.). *Campus 1980.* New York: Dell Publishing Co., 1968.

Featherstone, W.B. *A Functional Curriculum for Youth.* New York: American Book, 1950.

Felkin, Emmie and Henry M. *The Science of Education.* Boston: D. C. Heath & Co., 1893.

Fenster, C. B., and Perrett, M. C. *Behavior Principles.* New York: Appleton-Century-Crofts Division of Meredith Corporation, 1968.

Flagle, C. D., *et al.* (eds.) *Operations Research and Systems Engineering.* Baltimore: The Johns Hopkins Press, 1960.

Forest Service, U.S.D.A. *A Guide to Analyzing Instructional Needs.* Manual TT-7(6140). Washington, D.C.: U.S. Department of Agriculture.

Gage, N. I. (ed.). *Handbook on Research in Teaching.* Chicago: Rand McNally & Co., 1963.

Gagne, Robert M. *The Conditions of Learning.* New York: Holt, Rinehart & Winston, 1967.

Galbraith, John Kenneth. *The New Industrial State.* Boston: Houghton Mifflin, 1967.

Garrison, Roger H. (ed.). *Junior College Faculty: Issues and Problems.* Washington, D.C.: American Association of Junior Colleges, 1967.

Hall, A. D. *A Methodology for Systems Engineering.* New York: D. Van Nostrand, 1962.

Hirsch, Wirner Z. *et al. Inventing Education for the Future.* San Francisco: Chandler, 1967.

Husén, Thorsten (ed.). *International Study of Achievement in Mathematics,* Vol. I & II. New York: John Wiley, 1967.

Hutchens, Robert M. *The Conflict in Education in a Democratic Society.* New York: Harper & Co., 1953.

Johnson, B. Lamar. *Islands of Innovation Expanding: Changes in the Community College.* Beverly Hills, Cal.: Glencoe Press, 1969.

————. *Starting a Community Junior College.* Washington, D.C.: American Association for Junior Colleges, 1964.

————. *Systems Approaches to Curriculum and Instruction in the Open-Door College.* Los Angeles: University of California, 1967.

Judd, Charles Hubbard. *Introduction to the Scientific Study of Education.* Boston: Ginn & Co., 1918.

Kaufman, A. *Methods and Models of Operations Research.* Englewood Cliffs, N.J.: Prentice-Hall, 1963.

Kilpatrick, W. H. *The Project Method.* Teachers College, N.Y.: Columbia University Press, 1919.

Knirk, Frederick G., and Childs, John W. *Instructional Technology—A Book of Readings.* New York: Holt, Rinehart & Winston, 1968.

Kopstein, Felix F. *General Systems Theory as the Basis for a Theory of Instruction.* Research Memorandum 66-8 Princeton University: 1966.

————. *The Systems Approach to Education: An Introduction.* Princeton, N.J.: Educational Testing Service, 1966.

Kuhn, Thomas S. *The Structure of Scientific Revolutions.* Chicago: University of Chicago Press, 1962.

Likert, Rensis. *The Human Organization: Its Management and Value.* New York: McGraw-Hill, 1967.

Loughary, John W. *Man-Machine Systems in Education.* New York: Harper and Row, 1966.

McMurry, Charles. *How to Organize the Curriculum.* New York: Macmillan, 1923.

Mager, Robert F. and Kenneth N., Jr. *Developing Vocational Instruction.* Palo Alto: Fearon Publishers, 1967.

Markle, Susan Meyer. *Good Frames and Bad.* New York: John Wiley & Sons, Inc., 1966.

Melton, Arthur W. (ed.). *Categories of Human Learning.* New York: Academic Press, 1964.

Mesarovic, Mihajlo D. (ed.). *Views on General Systems Theory.* New York: John Wiley & Sons, Inc., 1964.

Monroe, Walter S., *et al. Ten Years of Educational Research, 1918-1927.* Urbana: University of Illinois, 1928.

Monroe, Walter S., and Engelhart, Max D. *The Scientific Study of Educational Problems.* New York: Macmillan Co., 1936.

Montessori, Maria. *The Montessori Method.* New York: Schocken Books, Inc., 1966.

O'Connor, Thomas J. *Follow-up Studies in Junior Colleges; A Tool for Institutional Improvement.* Washington, D.C.: American Association of Junior Colleges, 1965.

Optner, Stanford L. *Systems Analysis.* Englewood Cliffs, N.J.: Prentice-Hall, 1964.

Parker, Franklin. *The Junior and Community College: A Bibliography of Doctoral Dissertations.* Washington, D.C.: American Association of Junior Colleges, 1965.

Pavlov, I. P. *Conditioned Reflexes.* Translated by G. V. Anrep. London: Oxford University Press, 1927.

Peters, Charles C. *Foundations of Educational Sociology.* New York: The Macmillan Co., 1930.

Pfeiffer J. *New Look at Education: System Analysis in Our Schools and Colleges.* New York: Odyssey Press, 1968.

Postlethwait, S. N., Novak, J., and Murray, H. *An Integrated Experience Approach to Learning.* Minneapolis: Burgess Publishing Co., 1964.

Riendeau, Albert J. *The Role of the Advisory Committee in Occupational Education in the Junior College.* Washington, D.C.: American Association of Junior Colleges, 1967.

Roueche, John E. *A Bibliography of Doctoral Dissertations, 1964-1966.* Washington, D.C.: American Association of Junior Colleges, 1967.

————. *Junior College Institutional Research: the State of Art.* Washington, D.C.: American Association of Junior Colleges, 1968.

Rugg, Harold, ed. *Curriculum Making: Past and Present.* Twenty-sixth Yearbook, National Society for the Study of Education. Chicago: University of Chicago Press, 1926.

Rummler, Geary, *et al.* (*eds.*). *Managing the Instructional Programming Effort.* Ann Arbor: University of Michigan Press, 1967.

Schon, Donald A. *Technology and Change:* The New Heraclitus. New York: Delacorte Press, 1967.

Seguel, Mary Louise. *The Curriculum Field, Its Formative Years.* New York: Teachers College Press, 1966.

Siegel, Laurence. *Instruction, Some Contemporary Viewpoints.* San Francisco: Chandler Press, 1967.

Silvern, Leonard C. *Systems Engineering of Educations I: The Evolution of Systems Thinking in Education.* Los Angeles: Education and Training Consultants Co., 1971.

Silvern, Leonard C. *Systems Engineering of Learning—Public Education K-12: Vol. I. An Analysis; Vol. 2. A Synthesis.* Los Angeles: Univeristy of Southern California, 1965.

————. *Text Book in Methods of Instruction.* Fullerton, Cal. Hughes Aircraft Company, 1957, second printing 1962.

Skinner, B. F. *Walden Two*. New York: Macmillan, 1948.
————. *The Behavior of Organisms: An Experimental Analysis*. New York: Appleton-Century-Crofts, 1938.
————. *Science & Human Behavior*. New York: Macmillan, 1953.
————. *The Technology of Teaching*. New York: Appleton-Century-Crofts, 1968.
————. *Verbal Behavior*. New York: Appleton-Century-Crofts, 1957.
Smith, Eugene R., Tyler, Ralph W., and the Evaluation Staff. *Appraising and Recording Student Progress*. New York: Harper & Brothers, 1942.
Smith, Karl U., and Smith, Margaret Foltz. *Cybernetic Principles of Learning and Educational Design*. New York: Holt, Rinehart & Winston, 1966.
Snedden, David. *Problems of Educational Readjustment*. Boston: Houghton Mifflin, 1913.
————. *Sociological Determination of Objectives in Education*. Philadelphia: J. B. Lippincott, 1921.
Society for General Systems Research. *General Systems Yearbook of the Society for General Systems Research, 1956-1957, Vols. 1-12*. Bedford, Mass.: Society for General Systems Research, 1956-1967.
Stevenson, J. A. *The Project Method of Teaching*. New York: Macmillan, 1921.
Taba, Hilda. *Curriculum Development: Theory and Practice*. New York: Harcourt, Brace and World, 1962.
Thompson, James D. (ed.). *Approaches to Organizational Design*. 2nd ed., Pittsburgh: University of Pittsburgh Press, 1966.
Thorndike, E. L. *Animal Intelligence: Experimental Studies*. New York: Macmillan, 1911.
————. *Human Learning*. New York: Appleton-Century-Crofts, 1931.
Travers, Robert H.W. *Essentials of Learning: An Overview for Students of Education*. 2nd ed., New York: The Macmillan Co., 1967.
Tyler, Ralph W. *Basic Principles of Curriculum and Instruction*. Chicago: University of Chicago Press, 1949.
————. *Basic Principles of Curriculum Development*. Chicago: University of Chicago Press, 1950.
Tyler, Ralph W. (ed.). *Educational Evaluation: New Roles, New Means*. Sixty-eighth Yearbook, Part II. Chicago: University of Chicago Press, 1969.
U.S. Forest Service Manual, *A Guide to Analyzing Instructional Needs*. Washington, D.C.: Department of Agriculture, 11-7-(6140).
Washburne, Carleton W. *Adapting the Schools to Individual Differences*. Twenty-fourth Yearbook of the NSSE, Part II. Bloomington, Ill.: Public School Publishing Co., 1925.
Washburne, Carleton W., and Marland, Sidney P., Jr. *Winnetka: The History and Significance of an Educational Experiment*. Englewood Cliffs, N.J.: Prentice-Hall, 1963.
Wiener, Norbert. *Cybernetics; Or Control and Communication in the Animal and the Machine*. Cambridge, Mass.: MIT Press, 1961.
————. *The Human Use of Human Beings*. New York: Doubleday, A Doubleday Anchor Book, 1954.

ARTICLES AND PERIODICALS

Apter, Michael J. "Cybernetics and Its Relevance to Education."*Recall*—Review of Educational Cybernetics and Applied Linguistics, vol. 1, no. 1 (January 1969), 7-24.

Atkin, J. Myron. "Behavioral Objectives in Curriculum Design: A Cautionary Note," *Science Teacher,* 35:27-30 (May 1968).

Baldwin, Bird T. "The Present Status of Education as a Science." *School Review Monographs* (Chicago: University of Chicago Press, 1912), II, 119-134.

Barson, John. "Heuristics of Instructional Systems Development: A Team Report," *Audiovisual Instruction,* vol. 12, no. 6 (June-July 1967), 613-614.

Berkeley, Rice. Article in *New York Times Magazine,* March 17, 1968.

Bern, H. A., *et al.* "Reply to Questions about Systems," *Audiovisual Instruction,* vol. 10, no. 5 (May 1965), 360.

Bloom, Benjamin S. "Learning for Mastery." UCLA-CSEIP *Evaluation Comment I* (May 1968) (Center for the Study of Evaluation of Instructional Programs, 145 Moore Hall, 405 Hilgard, Los Angeles, Cal.).

————. "Twenty-five Years of Educational Research." *American Educational Research Journal* 3 (1966), 211-21.

Bobbitt, John Franklin. "Discovering and Formulating the Objectives of Teacher Training Institutions," *Journal of Educational Research* (October 1924).

Borton, Terry. "What Turns Kids On?" *Saturday Review,* 50:72-74, 80.

Burns, John L. "Our Era of Opportunity," *Saturday Review* (January 14, 1967), p. 39.

Canfield, Albert A. "Time for Instructional Research." *Junior College Research Review* 2 (December 1967).

Carpenter, C. R. "Approaches to Promising Areas of Research in the Field of Instructional Television." *New Teaching Aids* [*sic.*] *for the American Classroom,* The Institute for Communications Research, Stanford University, 1960, 75-76.

Charters, W. W. "Activity Analysis and Curriculum Construction." *Journal of Educational Research,* vol. 5 (May 1922), 357.

————. "Functional Analysis as the Basis for Curriculum Construction." *Journal of Educational Research* (October 1924).

————. "Idea Men and Engineers in Education." *The Educational Forum* (December 1951).

————. "Is There a Field of Educational Engineering?" *Educational Research Bulletin,* vol. 24, no. 2 (February 1945).

————. "The Era of the Educational Engineer." *Educational Research Bulletin* (December 1951).

Chestnut, H. "Automatic Control and Electronics." *Proceedings of the* IRE, Institute of Radio Engineers, New York (May 1962).

Ciancone, Elmer S. "New Technique for Instructional Analysis." *Industrial Arts & Vocational Education,* vol. 57, no. 4 (April 1968), 35.

Cohen, Harold L. "Educational Therapy: The Design of Learning Environments," and "Appendix A." *Research in Psychotherapy,* American Psychological Association, vol. 3 (1968), 21-53.

Cohodes, Aaron. "Using Systems Approach is Easier than Defining It." *Nation's Schools,* vol. 82 (August 1968), 16.

Davies, Ivor K. Introduction to "Review of Educational Cybernetics and Applied Linguistics," in *Recall,* Supplement 1 (March 1969).

————. "The Mathetics Style of Programming." *Programmed Learning and the Language Laboratory.* Collected papers. Klaus Bung, ed., Longmac, London, 1967.

Davis, Robert H. "The Heuristics of Learning System Design." Michigan State University, East Lansing, Michigan, Director Learning Service, (presented at Annual DAVI meeting in Houston, Texas), (March 1968).

Eash, Maurice J. "Is Systems Analysis for Supervisors?" *Educational Leadership,* 26 (February 1969), 482-487.

Eisner, Elliot W. "Educational Objectives: Help or Hindrance?" *School Review* 75: 250-60, 277-82, 1967.

Engler, David. "All Right, Computer, Explain the Systems Approach." *Nation's Schools,* vol. 80, no. 4 (October 1967), 57-59, 112.

Evans, J. L. "Programming in Mathematics and Logic." in R. Glaser (ed.): *Teaching Machines and Programmed Learning,* Department of Audio Visual Instruction, Washington, D.C., 1965.

Flanagan, John C. "Functional Education for the Seventies," *Phi Delta Kappan* vol. 49, no. 1 (September 1967), 27-32.

Flothaw, Rudolph C. "Systems Analysis and School Functions," *Education Digest,* 33 (January 1968), 27-30.

Forrester, J. W. "Common Foundations Underlying Engineering and Management." *IEEE Spectrum* (September 1964).

————. "Systems Technology and Industrial Dynamics." *MIT Technology Review* (June 1957).

Fuller, R. Buckminster. "Notes on the Future—The Prospect for Humanity." *Saturday Review* (August 29, 1964), 43-44, 180, 183.

Gagné, Robert M. "Science—A Process Approach." Commission on Science Education (September 1967), 1-16.

Gentile, J. Ronald. "The First Generation of Computer Assisted Instructional Systems: An Evaluative Review." *AV Communication Review,* vol. 10, no. 2 (March-April 1962), 75-84.

Gilbert, Thomas F. "Mathetics: The Technology of Education." *Journal of Mathetics,* University of Alabama, 1962 (as reprinted in *Recall,* Supplement 1, March 1969.

————. "Praxeonomy: A Systematic Approach to Identifying Training Needs." In *Management of Personnel Quarterly,* Bureau of Industrial Relations, University of Michigan, vol. 6, no. 3, 20-33.

Gilpin, John. "Design and Evaluation of Instructional Systems." *Audiovisual Communication Review,* vol. 10, no. 2 (March-April 1962), 75-84.

Goodlad, John I., ed. "Curriculum: State of the Field." *Review of Educational Research*, vol. 39, no. 3 (June 1969), 376-375.

———. "Toward a Conceptual System for Curriculum Problems." *School Review* 66 (Winter 1958), 391-396.

Hartley, Harry J. "Limitations of Systems Analysis." *Phi Delta Kappan*, (May 1969), 515-519.

Heinich, Robert. "The Systems Approach in Elementary and Secondary Education." Reviewed in *Audio Visual Instruction* (June-July 1966).

Hill, Edwin K., and Bergstrom, Phillip G. "Big Ideas for Small Schools." *Industrial Arts and Vocational Education*, vol. 57, no. 4. (April 1968), 6-15.

Hodges, Lewis C., and Gerald A. "Quickening the Pulse of Industrial Education." *School Shop*, vol. 27, no. 8 (April 1968), 68-71.

Homme, Lloyd E. "A Behavior Technology Exists—Here and Now," in *Technology and Innovation in Education*, Aerospace Education Foundation, New York: Praeger, 1968.

"Innovation: Urban Problems Need Systems Approach." *School and Society*, 96 (Summer 1968), 277.

Judd, Charles H. "The Scientific Technique of Curriculum Making." *School and Society*, vol. 15, no. 367 (January 1922).

Kapfer, Philip C. "An Instructional Management Strategy for Individualized Learning."*PDK*, vol. 49 (January 1968).

Kliebard, Herbert. "Curricular Objectives and Evaluation: A Reassessment." *High School Journal*, 51:241-47, 1968.

Knirk, Frederick G. "Analysis of Instructional Systems: A Reaction." *Audiovisual Instruction* (October 1965).

Lieberman, Myron. "Big Business, Technology and Education." *Phi Delta Kappan* (January 1967).

Locke, Edwin A. "Motivational Effects of Knowledge of Results." *American Institute for Research*, Washington Office, 1967.

Loughary, J. W. "Instructional Systems—Magic or Method?" *Educational Leadership*, 25, 1968, 730-734.

Meals, Donald W. "Heuristic Models for Systems Planning." *Phi Delta Kappan*, vol. 47, no. 5 (January 1967), 199-203.

Miescicki, Jerry, and Muszyński, Msciwaj. "A Way to Optimal Textbooks." *Poland* (July 1969), 3-5.

Miller, Aaron J. "Research Priorities in Technical Teacher Education; A Planning Model." Center for Research and Leadership Development in Vocational & Technical Education. (Columbus, Ohio: The Ohio State University, October 1967), 30.

Morris, B. (ed.). "The Function of Media in the Public Schools." *Audiovisual Instruction* (January 1963).

Moss, Jerome. "Review of Research in Vocational Technical Teacher Education." Minnesota Research Coordination Unit in Occupational Education, (Minneapolis: University of Minnesota, September 1967), 26.

McMorris, Robert F. "National Assessment: Coming in 1968-69." *Phi Delta Kappan* 49:599-600, 1968.

McNeil, John D. "Forces Influencing Curriculum." AERA *Review of Educational Research* (April 1968), 303.

Naber, Richard. "Dial for Education Information." *Audio Visual Instruction* (December 1968), 1,082-85.

"New Systems Approaches to H-V-AC." American School and University, 41 (January 1969), 31-32.

Oettinger, Anthony G. "The Myths of Educational Technology." *Saturday Review* 51:76-77, 91 (May 18, 1968).

Ofiesh, Gabriel D. "Tomorrow's Educational Engineers." *Educational Technology* (July 15, 1968), p. 5.

Parker, Stephenson. "PPBS." *California Teachers Association Journal,* 65 (May 1969), 9-11.

Pask, G. "Adaptive Teaching with Adaptive Machines," in *Teaching Machines and Programmed Learning,* Lumsdaine and Glaser, eds. Washington, D.C.: Department of Audiovisual Instruction, National Education Association, 1960.

Persselin, Leo E. "Systems Implications for Secondary Education." *Journal of Secondary Education,* 44 (April 1969), 159-165.

Phipps, Lloyd J., and Evans, Rupert N. "Curriculum Development." *Review of Educational Research* 38:367-381, 1968.

Poorman, Lawrence Eugene. "A Comparative Study of the Effectiveness of Multi-Media Systems Approach to Harvard Project Physics with Traditional Approaches to Harvard Project Physics." *Educational Resource Information Center,* vol. 4, no. 6 (June 1969), 83.

Riley, J. W., and Riley, M. W. "Sociological Perspectives on the Use of New Educational Media." *New Teaching Aids for the Classroom: A Symposium on the State of Research in Instructional Television and Tutorial Machines,* Stanford, Cal., Stanford University Press, 1959.

Roueche, John E. "Gaps and Overlaps in Institutional Research." *Junior College Journal* 38:20-23 (November 1967).

Russo, Michael. "Concepts and Procedures for Systematic Planning of Vocational Facilities." *American Vocational Journal,* 44 (January 1969), 23-24.

Ryan, T. Antoinette. "Systems Techniques for Programs of Counseling and Counselor Education." *Educational Technology,* vol. 9, no. 6 (June 1969).

Saettler, Paul. "Instructional Technology: Some Concerns and Desiderata." *AV Communication Review,* vol. 17, no. 4 (Winter 1969), DAVI-NEA, Washington, D.C., p. 359.

Scates, Douglas E. "Judd and the Scientific Study of Education." *The School Review,* vol. 75 (1967), 2-28.

Schutz, Richard E. "Experimentation Relating to Formative Evaluation." *Research & Development Strategies in Theory Refinement and Educational Improvement.* Theoretical Paper No. 15, Madison: University of Wisconsin Research & Development Center for Cognitive Learning, 1968, pp. 19-22.

"Science Curriculum Program: Implementation of Science—A Process Approach."*Sixth Report of the International Clearinghouse on Science and Mathematics Curricular Developments* (1968), p. 395.

Sergeant, Harold A. "Development and Testing of An Experimental Polysensory Instructional System for Teaching Electric Arc Welding Process." *Educational Resource Information Center,* vol. 4, no. 2 (February 1969), 138.

Showalter, Victor. "New Directions for Science Curriculum Development." *Educational Resource Information Center,* vol. 4, no. 6 (June 1969), 36.

Silvern, Leonard C. "A Cybernetic System Model for Occupational Education." *Educational Technology* (January 30, 1968).

————. "Guide to the State Fire Training Program." State Division of Safety, Albany, N.Y. (1951).

————. "Studies in the Systems Engineering of Education, I: Basic Data on the Evolution of Systems Thinking in Education." In *Instructional Technology and Media Project* (Los Angeles: School of Education, University of Southern California, 1971).

————. "Introduction." *Educational Technology,* vol. 9, no. 6 (June 1969).

Skinner, B. F. "Are Theories of Learning Necessary?" *Psychology Review* (1950), 57.

Stolurow, L. M. "Teaching by Machine." U.S. Department of Health, Education and Welfare, *Cooperative Research,* Monograph OE34010, no. 6 (1961).

Stufflebeam, Daniel. "A Depth Study of the Evaluation Requirement." *Theory into Practice* 5:121-33 (1966).

Suppes, Patrick. "The Computer & Excellence." *Changing Directions in American Education.* In *Saturday Review* (January 14, 1967).

Systems Analysis Committee. "A Proposal for Long-Range Educational Analysis and Planning." *Educational Media Council,* New York, N.Y. (September 16, 1963).

"Systems Design and Nature of Work (Seminar on Manpower Policy and Program, Washington, D.C., November 17, 1966)." *Educational Resource Information Center,* vol. 4, no. 4 (April 1969), 118.

Tanner, Kenneth C. "Techniques and Application of Educational Systems Analysis." *Audiovisual Instruction,* 14 (March 1969), 89-90.

Tirrell, John. "Some Reflections on 150 Man-Years. Using the Systems Approach in an Open-Door College." Occasional paper, B. Lamar Johnson, ed., University of California at Los Angeles, 1967, pp. 57-58.

Tischler, Morris. "Systems Approach—Modern Technology in Skills Training." *Industrial Arts and Vocational Education,* vol. 57, no. 9 (November 1968), 31-33.

Tracy, William R. *et. al.* "Systems Approach Gets Results." *Training in Business and Industry* (June 1967).

Ulrich, Bernard. "A Training Model for the Jobless Adult." *Educational Resource Information Center,* vol. 3, no. 9 (September 1968), 12.

Watson, Paul G. "Instructional Strategies & Learning Systems." *Audiovisual Instruction,* vol. 13, no. 8 (October 1968), 843-846.

Weltner, Klaus, "Information Theory and Programmed Instruction." *RECALL—Review of Educational Cybernetics and Applied Linguistics,* vol. 1, no. 1 (January 1969), 25-41.

"What Is a Planning, Programming, Budgeting System?" *National Education Association Research Bulletin,* 46 (December 1968), 112-113.

Wolfe, Arthur B. "Nova's Technical Science Program." *Industrial Arts and Vocational Education,* vol. 56, no. 6. (June 1967), 31-33.

Wolfle, D. "Training." *Handbook of Experimental Psychology* (1951). By permission of John Wiley & Sons, Inc.

Worlton, J. T. "Selecting Curriculum Content." *Journal of National Education Association,* vol. 25 (November 1936), 238.

Yoho, Lewis W. "The 'Orchestrated System' Approach to Industrial Education." Industrial Arts, Technical, Vocational," *Educational Resource Information Center,* vol. 3, no. 11 (November 1968), 142.

REPORTS

"An Instructional Systems Approach to Physical and Earth Sciences." *Sixth Report of the International Clearinghouse on Science and Mathematics Curricular Development* (1968), 392.

Atkinson, J. W., and O'Connor, P. "Effects of Ability Grouping in Schools Related to Individual Differences in Achievement-Related Motivation." U S. Office of Education, Cooperative Research Program, Project 1283, University of Michigan (1963).

Baker, Robert L., and Schultz, Richard E. *Technical Documentary: Research on Procedures for the Revision of Instructional Materials,* Wright-Patterson Air Force Base, Ohio: Aerospace Medical Division, Air Force Systems Command (1967).

Bobbitt, John Franklin. *Denver School Survey—Report of the School Survey of School District #1 in the City and County of Denver, Colorado,* The School Survey Committee (1916).

Bruner, Jerome S. "Theorems for a Theory of Instruction." *Learning About Learning; A Conference Report,* edited by Jerome Bruner, Director for Cognitive Studies—Harvard Cooperative Research Monograph No .15, Washington, D.C.: United States Government Printing Office, 1966.

Cogswell, J. F., Bratten, J. E., Egbert, R. E., Eslavan, D. P., Marsh, D. G., and Yett, F. A. *Analysis of Instructional Systems.* Final Report, OE 7-14-9120-217, Santa Monica, Cal.: S.D.C. (1966).

Cogswell, John F. "The Systems Approach as a Heuristic Method in Educational Development, An Application to the Counseling Function." Santa Monica, Cal.: Systems Development Corporation, March 5, 1962, SP-720.

Cohen, Harold. "Motivationally Oriented Designs for an Ecology of Learning." Silver Spring, Md.: Institute for Behavioral Research, 1967.

Cohen, Harold, Filipczak, James, Bix, John. "Case I (An Initial Study of Contingencies Applicable to Special Education)." Silver Spring, Md., Institute for Behavioral Research, 1967.

Conference on Junior College Libraries. *Development Needs and Perspective* College Libraries, University of California, Los Angeles, 1967.

"Cubberley-Lockheed Science Project Final Report, Volume III, Phase II System Specifications." *Educational Resource Information Center,* vol. 4, no. 6 (June 1969), 84.

Department of Defense, Office of Education and NSIA. *Education Systems for Education and Training,* Proceedings of Conference on Education Systems for Education and Training (June 1966).

Egbert, R. L., and Cogswell, J. F. "System Design in the Bassett High School." TM-1147, Santa Monica, Cal.: Systems Development Corporation (April 1963).

————. "Systems Design for Continuous Progress School: Parts I & II," Santa Monica, Cal.: Systems Development Corporation (1964).

Glaser, Robert. *Theory of Evaluation of Instruction: Changes and Trends.* From the Proceedings of the Symposium on Problems in the Evaluation of Instruction, December 1967. CSEIP Occasional Report No. 13, Los Angeles: University of California, Center for the Study of Instructional Programs.

Johnson, B. Lamar. *Systems Approaches to Curriculum and Instruction in the Open-Door College,* Occasional Report from University of Southern California, Junior College Leadership Program #9, January 1967, Los Angeles: University of California Regents.

Lehmann, Henry. *8 Steps in the Design of an Education and Training System.* Prepared by Task Groups on the Systems Approach to Education & Training, Washington, D.C.: NSIA, Project Aristotle Symposium (December 1967).

Kershaw, Joseph A., and McKean, Roland N. *Systems Analysis and Education,* Santa Monica, Cal.: The Rand Corporation, 1959.

National Conference on New Directions for Instruction in the Junior College, University of California 1964.

"New Dimensions for Research in Educational Media Implied by the 'Systems' Approach to Instruction." Center for Instructional Communications, Syracuse University (April 1964), 2-4.

Ofiesh, Gabriel D. "Results of an Air Force Study of Programmed Instruction." Remarks at a symposium of Division 19 (military psychology), American Psychological Association Annual Conference, 4 September 1963.

O'Toole, John F., Jr. *Systems Analysis and Decision-Making in Education* Santa Monica, Cal.: Systems Development Corporation (1965).

Rhode, W. E., Esseff, P. J., Pusin, C. J., *et al. Instructional System Study: Guidelines for the Selection of a Multimedia Configuration and the Design of a Management Information System for Individualized Instruction.* Westinghouse Learning Corporation, Training Systems Division, Preliminary Draft (February 1970).

Smith, Robert G., Jr. *The Design of Instructional Systems.* Technical Report 66-18 of the Human Resources Research Office (HumRRO), Washington, D.C.: George Washington University, (November 1966).

Stolurow, L. M. "Some Educational Problems and Prospects of a Systems Approach to Instruction." From Conference, "New Dimensions for Research in Educational Media Implied by the 'Systems' Approach to Instruction," Center for Instructional Communications, Syracuse University (April 1964), 2-4.

————. *Systems Approach to Instruction.* Technical Report No. 7, Urbana, Ill.: Training Research Laboratory, University of Illinois (July 1965).

System Planning Workshop, Headquarters Air Training Command, Randolph Air Force Base (June 1964).

United States National Commission on Technology, Automation and Economic Progress, Report, Washington, D.C. (February 1966).

University of Southern California Occasional Report #9, Los Angeles, 1967, p. 5.

UNPUBLISHED MATERIAL

Barbee, David E., and Motzel, L. William. "Core Objective #1—A Systems Approach to the Design of Instructional Systems," The Catholic University, Washington, D.C., 1968.

Colorado Mountain College. Status Study for NCA, April 1969.

————. Official Minutes of Governing Committee, 1966-1969.

————. "Colorado Mountain College: An Adventure in Modern Learning." Unpublished paper, 1966.

————. "Statement of Philosophy and Methodology for Colorado Mountain College." Unpublished paper, 1966.

The Continuation Education System Development Project, Leon East, project director, La Puente, Calif., unpublished brief description, n.d.

Evans, James L. "The Technology of Doing Your Own Thing—A Nonpaper on the Nonfuture of Noneducation." The Seventh Annual Convention of the National Society for Programmed Instruction, Washington, D.C., April 1969.

Gilbert, Thomas F. "Mathetical Performance Analysis." Unpublished booklet, Praxeonomy Institute Inc., 276 Riverside Drive, New York, N.Y. 10025.

Hammerel, Mary Ann. "Use of Incentives in Learning." Unpublished paper for the Study of Instructional Technology at Catholic University of America, Washington, D.C., n.d.

Hammerel, Mary Ann, and Laidlaw, W. J. Report prepared for the Study of Instructional Technology, Academy for Educational Development, Inc., n.d.

Heinich, Robert. "A System of Instructional Management." Unpublished paper, November 1962. Later amplified in *Technology and the Management of Instruction,* Association for Educational Communications and Technology, 1970.

Henderson, William M. "The Analysis Mystique." Unpublished paper, Indiana University, Nov. 1962.

Homme, Lloyd E. "Behavioral Engineering in Instructional Systems." Paper presented at the Minuteman Instructional Systems Planning Conference, Autonetics, Anaheim, Calif., November 6, 1964.

Postlethwait, S. N. "Instructional Techniques" (abstract). Purdue University, unpublished, undated paper.

Schwab, Joseph J. "The Practical: A Language for Curriculum." Unpublished address, Annual Conference of the American Educational Research Association, February 1969, Chicago: University of Chicago, School of Education.

Stewart, Donald K. "A Learning Systems Concept as Applied to Courses in Education and Training (Pamphlet), College Station, Texas, Center for Creative Application of Technology to Education.

Suchesk, Arthur M. "Southern California Regional Occupational Center A New Environment for Industrial Education." Presented at the Second Annual National Laboratory for the Advancement of Education, Washington Hilton Hotel, January 1970.

Tirrell, John. "Program Innovation." Paper presented to the Council of North Central Junior College, Denver, Colorado, October 3, 1966.

OTHER SOURCES

Gleazer, Edmund J., Jr. "The Community College, What Is It—A New Social Invention;" undated brochure of the American Association of Junior Colleges, Washington, D.C. (1965?).

Hammerel, Mary Ann, and Laidlaw, W. J. "Instructional Technology and the Job Corps Curriculum." An unpublished paper prepared for the Study of Instructional Technology Academy for Educational Development Inc., undated (1968?)

Mechner, Francis, and Cook, Donald A."Behavior Technology and Manpower Development." Background paper prepared for the Organization for Economic Cooperation and Development by Basic Systems, New York, New York, 1964.

Patty, William Lovell. A Study of mechanism in Education; an Examination of the curriculum-making devices of Franklin Bobbitt, W. W. Charters, and C. C. Peters from the point of view of relativistic Pragmatism. New York, T. C. Columbia University, 1938.

Phipps, John. "Applications of the Systems Sciences in the Design and Development of Large Automated Instructional Systems." Dissertation, 1969.

Silvern, L. C. "Fundamentals of Teaching Machine and Programmed Learning Systems." A programmed course: Education and Training Consultants Co., Los Angeles, California; February 1964.

Smith, Robert G., Jr. "Controlling the Quality of Training." Technical Report 65-6, June 1965, Washington D.C.

————. "The Development of Training Objectives," Research Bulletin, June 11, 1964.

United States Air Force. "Programmed Learning," Air Force Manual No. 50-1, United States Air Force; 31 July 1964.

The Model—reprinted

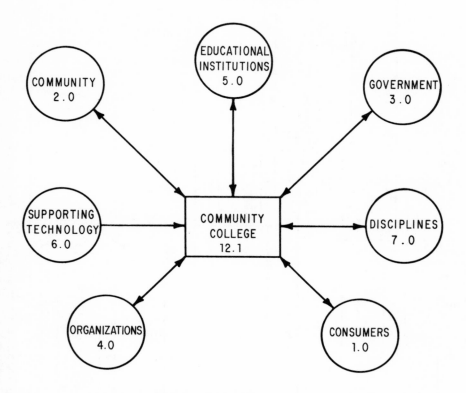

Figure 5-15.   The Model: Community College—Inputs
from Other Systems.

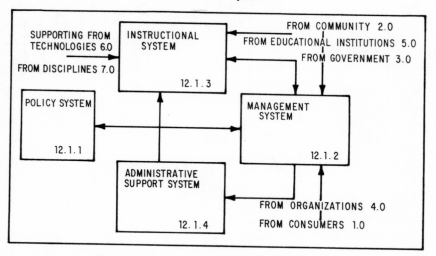

Figure 5-16.   The Model: Community College.

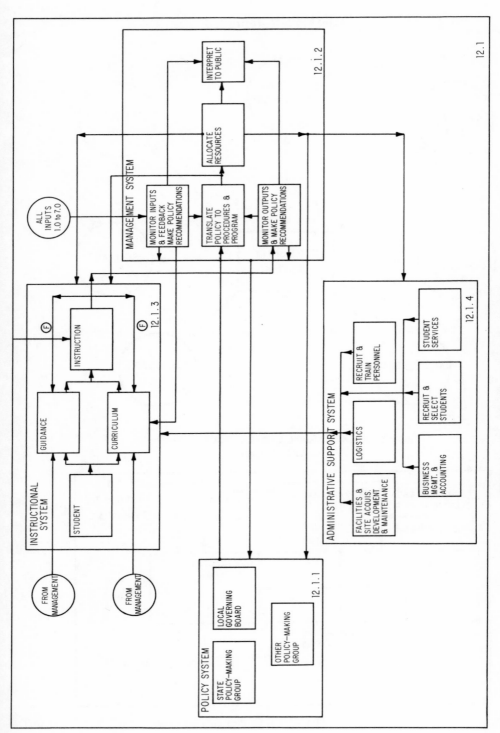

Figure 5-17. The Model: Community College—Relationship of Functions, Inputs, and Outputs.

176

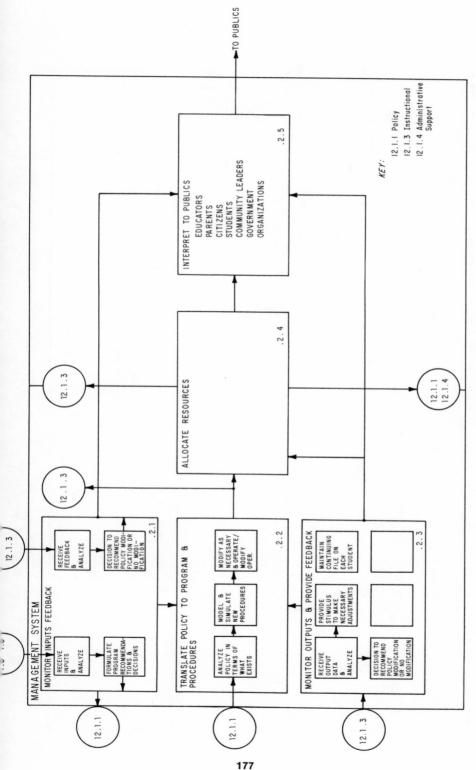

Figure 5-18.   The Model: Community College—the Management System.

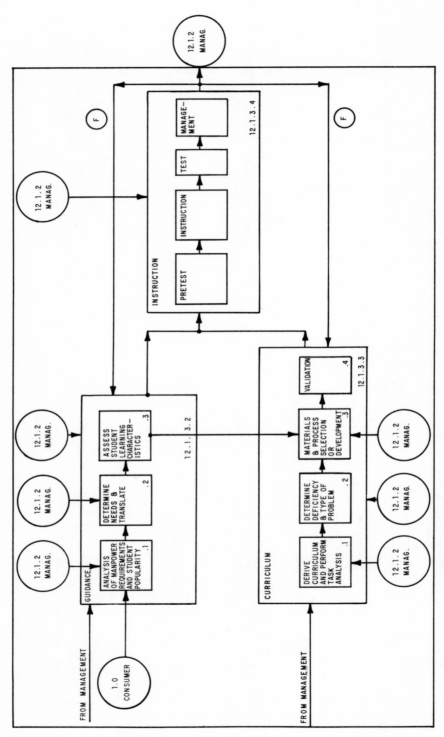

Figure 5-19. The Model: Community College—the Instructional System.

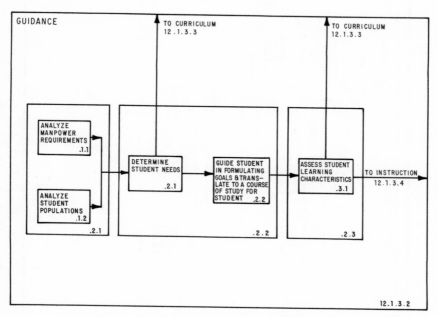

Figure 5-20.   The Model: Community College—Guidance.

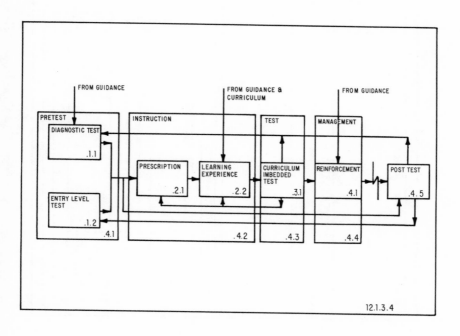

Figure 5-22.   The Model: Community College—Instruction.

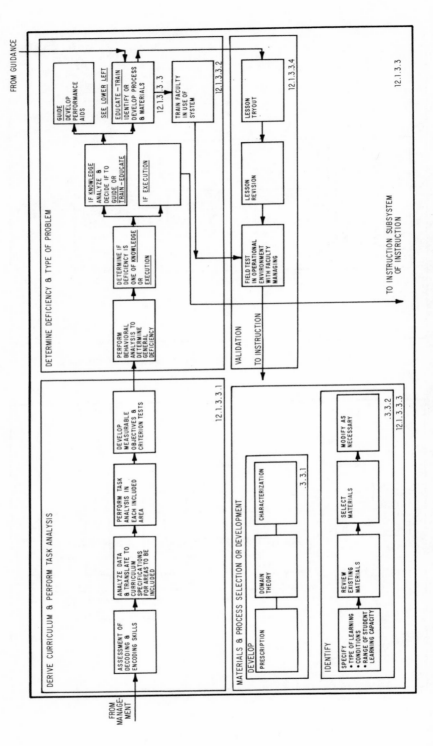

Figure 5-21. The Model: Community College—The Curriculum.

Index